Warning Out in New England 1656-1817

Josiah Henry Benton

HERITAGE BOOKS
2008

HERITAGE BOOKS
AN IMPRINT OF HERITAGE BOOKS, INC.

Books, CDs, and more—Worldwide

For our listing of thousands of titles see our website at
www.HeritageBooks.com

Published 2008 by
HERITAGE BOOKS, INC.
Publishing Division
100 Railroad Ave. #104
Westminster, Maryland 21157

Copyright © 1911 Josiah Henry Benton

All rights reserved. No part of this book may be reproduced or transmitted in any form or by any means, electronic or mechanical, including photocopying, recording or by any information storage and retrieval system without written permission from the author, except for the inclusion of brief quotations in a review.

International Standard Book Numbers
Paperbound: 978-1-55613-730-3
Clothbound: 978-0-7884-7118-6

TABLE OF CONTENTS.

	PAGE
CHAPTER 1. Introduction.—Examples of Warning Out.—Inhabitancy.—Land Titles in New England	1–17
CHAPTER 2. Admission of Inhabitants.—Grants of Land by Towns.—Restraint of Alienation of Lands.—Proceedings in Boston and Other Massachusetts and Plymouth Towns.	18–45
CHAPTER 3. Massachusetts Colony and State Laws.—Plymouth Colony Laws.—Further Illustrations of Town Action as to Inhabitancy, Alienation of Land, Warning Out, etc.	46–62
CHAPTER 4. Inhabitancy and Warning Out in Connecticut.—Early Colony and State Laws.—Illustrations of Action of Towns, etc.	63–87
CHAPTER 5. New Hampshire Colony and State Laws.—Action of Towns as to Inhabitancy, Warning Out, Relief of the Poor, etc.	88–98
CHAPTER 6. Rhode Island Colony and State Laws as to Inhabitancy, Relief of the Poor, Town Settlement, etc.—Maine and Vermont State Laws as to Warning Out, Inhabitancy, Settlement, Relief of the Poor, etc.	99–113
CHAPTER 7. The Length of Time Warning Out was practised.—Effect of Warning Out, How Avoided.—Value of Warning Out Records.—Summary as to Reasons for Warning Out, etc.	114–121
CHRONOLOGY	122
INDEX	123–131

CHAPTER I.

INTRODUCTION.—EXAMPLES OF WARNING OUT.—INHABITANCY.—LAND TITLES IN NEW ENGLAND.

The information contained in this book was gathered in the preparation of a paper read before the New England Historic-Genealogical Society. The paper was not printed, because it was thought the subject was of sufficient general interest to warrant its presentation in a book for the use of the public at large. This volume has therefore no claim to merit except that it contains material which has not before been brought together, relating to an interesting chapter in the Colonial and early State history of New England.

I have attempted to tell the story mainly in the language of the records and statutes of the time. I believe that real history is thus best written. As the eminent historian of New England so well said:—

> The peculiar language of the men whom the historian describes is a substantive part of their peculiar history. It displays the form and pressure of the place and time. The phraseology of the actors is a constant expositor and reminder of the complexion of the thoughts and sentiments that determined the course of affairs.*

In the records of the town of Alstead, New Hampshire, is found this:—

STATE OF NEW HAMPSHIRE, CHESHIRE SS.
    To SAML. KIDDER one of the Constables of Alstead,
Greeting:
IN the name of the Government & people of said state you are hereby Required forthwith to warn Jacob Benton & Hannah his wife, Mabel, Jacob, Reynold, Mary & Samuel Benton, their children to Depart out of this Town Immediately & no longer make

---

* Palfrey, *History of New England*, Vol. I, p. xvi.

it the place of their Residence under the pains that will follow. Hereof fail not & make Return of this warrant with your doings thereon as soon as may be.

Given under our hands and seal of office this 26th March 1783.

April 7, 1783

AMOS SHEPARD
TIMO FLETCHER } Selectmen.
SIMON BROOKS, Jr.

Serv^d. this warrant by reading the same in the hearing of s^d persons

SAML. KIDDER
Const.

The Jacob Benton named in this notice was my great-grandfather, and the Samuel, who was then about five years old, was my grandfather.

In the records of the town of Rockingham, Vermont, there is found this:—

STATE OF VERMONT, } To either Constable of Rockingham in
WINDHAM COUNTY ss } the County of Windham.   *Greeting.*

You are hereby required to summon Joseph Bellows and Mary Bellows his wife and George Bellows, Henry A. Bellows and Fanny A. Bellows, their children, now residing in Rockingham to depart s'd Town.

Hereof fail not, but of this precept & your doings herein due return make according to law.

Given under our hands at Rockingham this 30 day of May 1813.

JONATHAN BARRON } Selectmen
SAM'L W. PULSIPHER } of
ELIAS OLCOTT   } Rockingham

The return upon this warrant was that it had been served "by putting a true and attested copy into the hands of the within named Joseph Bellows with this my return endorsed thereon."

In 1791 this warrant was issued in Lancaster, Massachusetts:—

You are directed to warn and give notice unto the Hon. John Sprague, late of Rochester, in the County of Plymouth, Esq., a sheriff of the County of Worcester, John Maynard, late of Fram-

Warning Out in New England 3

ingham, in the County of Middlesex, Esq., Edmund Heard, late of Worcester, in the County of Worcester, Esq., Ebenezer Torrey, late of Boston, in the County of Suffolk, gentleman; William Stedman, late of Cambridge, in the County of Middlesex, Esq., Merrick Rice, late of Brookfield, in the County of Worcester, gentleman, Joseph Wales, late of Braintree, in the County of Suffolk, gentleman, who have lately come into this town for the purpose of abiding therein, not having obtained the town's consent therefor, that they respectively depart the limits thereof, with their children and all under their care within 15 days.

Upon reading these records, we are naturally led to inquire why these persons were thus summarily notified to leave their homes and depart out of the towns in which they lived. The notices themselves give no reason, and there was no reason in the character of the persons, why they should be thus treated. My great-grandfather was a good soldier, a devout Christian, and a peaceable citizen. Joseph Bellows was a distinguished soldier, a charming man, and an excellent citizen. He had moved from Walpole, New Hampshire, across the Connecticut River, to Rockingham, Vermont, to a new farm, and was a desirable addition to the population of the town. Henry A. Bellows, one of the persons named among his children, and warned out, was Henry Adams Bellows, who became an eminent lawyer, and was for many years the chief justice of the State of New Hampshire. The persons named in the Lancaster warrant were all desirable and excellent citizens. Obviously, none of these were persons whom the citizens desired to have depart out of their towns. Why, therefore, were they thus summarily warned to depart? What was the reason of this apparently extraordinary and unjust treatment of these persons? The treatment was, of course, authorized by law; but why was there such a law? What was the reason for it?

property in a city. . . . Every person who has land and house, who are called "householders," ought to be in frankpledge, and also others who serve them, who are called "followers." He is of the household and family of any one who has food and clothing from him, or who has food only with wages such as are the domestics or servitors and hirelings of the house.

Likewise according to ancient custom he may be said to be of any one's family who has dwelt in the house of another person for three nights, because on the first night he may be termed uncuth [unknown] but on the second gust [i.e., guest] on the third night hoghenehgue [or his own hind.]*

Upon this obligation to be in frankpledge, all freemen below a certain rank in England were, after the Danish conquest, required to be numbered in groups of ten, called tithings, and each member of a tithing made responsible for the good behavior of every other member.†

This responsibility was at first, by custom only, for a payment in money to the persons injured by crime, or to his relatives in case he was killed, and for a fine to be paid to the king as a punishment for the crime.‡

From this communal responsibility, and from the division of land under the feudal system, as perfected and extended throughout England after the Norman conquest,§ the civil institutions and the law of England were developed.

The local and municipal development of government in England was: first, from the hundred; second, from the tithings; third, from the parish, or ville, or town. The parish was originally intended for secular purposes

---

* Bracton, *De Legibus Angliæ*, edition 1879, Vol. II, p. 307.

† Pike, *History of Crime in England*, Vol. I, p. 58.

‡ Stephen, *Criminal Law of England*, p. 10.

§ "Of all the feudal services enforced by the Normans, there is not perhaps one of which some obscure trace may not be discovered among the Anglo-Saxons." Lingard, *History of England*, Vol. I, p. 488 (5th edition).

only, and was responsible for the maintenance of the public peace and for the support of the poor.*

In 1628 Lord Coke defined a town as follows:—

> It cannot be a town in law, unless it hath, or in past time hath had, a church, and celebration of divine services, sacraments and burial.

Blackstone in 1765 said,—

> Tithings, towns or villes, are of the same signification in law; and are said to have had each of them, originally, a church and celebration of divine service, sacraments and burials, though that seems to be rather an ecclesiastical than a civil distinction.†

A later English writer says,—

> The township is now known by its ecclesiastical name of parish, and the shire by its Norman name of county, but the old identity is still preserved, and the institutions themselves are as much alive today as they were a thousand years ago.

Again the same writer says:—

> The original unit of settlement among the Saxons in England was the tun, now town. This meant simply an enclosure surrounded by a wall or hedge, and the township was merely the area claimed by the town.

In the process of the English civil wars responsible local government practically disappeared, and in the general break-up of local conditions a question of very great magnitude arose, which was the relief of the poor. There was no local machinery available for this and it was taken up by the parish, which became the poor-law unit; that is, the church assumed the duty of looking after the poor, which had always been one of its primary duties, and hence the poor-law officials were elected by the parish vestry, which levied taxes

---

* Toulmin Smith, *The Parish*, pp. 16, 44, 45.
† Blackstone, *Commentaries*, Vol. I, p. 115.

for the support of the poor upon the householders of the parish.

In 1601, the date of the first great poor law of England, the parish or township began to revive as the machinery of local government and highways, bridges, drainage, police, education, and other local matters became parochial, and the old powers of the town meeting were resumed.*

It was upon this foundation of English affairs that the settlers of New England constructed their town or local governments.

Inhabitancy and "warning out" in the New England States were so connected that neither can be intelligently considered without examination of the other.

The theory of the early settlers with regard to inhabitancy was thus stated in the beginning:—

> If we here be a corporation, established by free consent, if the place of our co-habitation be our own, then no man hath right to come in to us without our consent.

Inhabitancy, or the right to live in a town as one of its inhabitants, did not necessarily include the right to vote in town affairs, nor was it always dependent upon the ownership of land. For instance, in the Massachusetts Colony the right to vote was confined by colony ordinance in 1631 to those inhabitants who were in full church communion, which put the government into the hands of a minority of the male inhabitants.†

In Plymouth and in Connecticut the franchise was given by vote of the freemen of the towns, but the candidate was required to be "of sober and peaceable

---

* Jenks, *English Local Government*, pp. 11, 19, 23, 28.
† *Massachusetts Colony Records*, Vol. I, p. 87.

conversation, orthodox in the fundamentals of religion and to have at least twenty pounds of rateable estate." *

It is true the word "inhabitants" was sometimes used as though it meant persons entitled to vote, as where the record speaks of a town meeting as a general meeting of the inhabitants, but I use it here as meaning simply persons who had been, by some general law or by the action of the town itself, admitted to be permanent residents in the town. This right of inhabitancy included by the common law of England the right to be supported by the town, if the inhabitant became unable to support himself. In other words, a legal inhabitancy comprehended a legal settlement, which in England could be acquired by residence in a place for a required period, originally forty days.†

This responsibility of municipalities for the proper conduct and for the support of their inhabitants, when they were unable to support themselves, properly implied the right to exclude from inhabitancy persons for whose conduct or support they did not desire to become responsible. In this is found the effective meaning of "giving the freedom of the city"; that is, the right to inhabit or dwell in the city. This also is the origin of the liability of municipalities for property destroyed in riots, which still exists by statute in many cases.‡

It is probably also the origin of the common law of the New England States, derived from immemorial usage, that the estate of any inhabitant of a town is liable to be taken in execution on a judgment against the town.§

* *Plymouth Colony Laws* (Brigham edition), 1671, p. 258; *Connecticut Colony Records*, Vol. I, pp. 290, 297, 331, 389, 417.
† Blackstone, *Commentaries*, Vol. I, p. 362.
‡ *General Laws of Rhode Island*, 1909, Chap. 344, Sect. 10; *Massachusetts Laws*, 1839, Chap. 54, Sects. 2, 3; *Revised Laws of Massachusetts*, Chap. 211, Sect. 8.
§ *Hill v. Boston*, 122 Mass. 349; *Beardsley v. Smith*, 16 Conn. 368.

This right of the towns to exclude from inhabitancy within their limits was undoubtedly exercised in the New England Colonies of New Plymouth, Massachusetts Bay, Connecticut, and even in Rhode Island, for the purpose of keeping out persons whose religious or political opinions were unsatisfactory to the towns. But the *reason for the existence* of this right was that inhabitancy, or the right to live in a place, always imposed upon the inhabitants of the place responsibility for the good conduct and support of the inhabitant.

The right to live in a town was then understood to imply a right to have land upon which to live, and therefore, when towns admitted persons to be inhabitants, they impliedly agreed to allot to them land upon which they could live as inhabitants from the town lands, and to give them the right of commonage in the common lands of the town. This also carried with it the right of free fishing and fowling in the great ponds and in the rivers and tidal-waters within the limits of the town.* In some cases, however, this right of commonage was restricted by the town in case of new-comers. In Boston it was ordered on May 18, 1648, at a town meeting that all inhabitants who had been admitted by the townsmen should have equal "Rights of Commonage in the towne," but that no one who should thereafter come to be an inhabitant in the town should have "right of Commonage" "unlese he hier it of them that are Commoners."† In Dorchester on January 18, 1635, it was ordered

that all the hoame lots within Dorchester Plantation which have bene granted before this p'sent day shall have right to the

---

* *Body of Liberties*, 1641; *Massachusetts Laws*, 1660–1672 (Whitmore edition), p. 37.

† *Boston Town Records*, 1634–1660, p. 88.

Commons and no other lotts that are graunted hereafter to be commoners: Also that Two men shall not Common for one hoame lott.*

At first it was not the practice to admit persons as inhabitants to whom the town could not allot lands upon which they could live. But it soon became the practice to admit them, provided they could, with the consent of the town, purchase land of other inhabitants to whom land had previously been allotted. The New England colonists not only had the Saxon greed for land, but their government was based upon the ownership of land, so far as possible, by all the inhabitants. They believed, and rightly, that nothing was so sure to give people an interest in sound and stable government as the ownership of their homes. They sought therefore to secure in some way to all the inhabitants of the towns an ownership in land, either by giving them lands owned by the towns or by requiring them to purchase lands in the towns before they became inhabitants. It will be seen therefore that a knowledge of inhabitancy in the early New England towns, and of the obligation of the inhabitants for the good conduct and support of each other, requires some reference to the origin of land titles in New England.

The basis of these titles was a grant from the English Crown. It is true that deeds of land were taken from the Indians, and that they were upheld by the Colonial Courts in some cases.†

It is also the fact that the original title taken by the settlers or planters of Rhode Island was by Indian grants, and that the early settlers of Connecticut also purchased their lands from the Indians in the

---

* *Dorchester Town Records*, p. 14.
† Sullivan, *Land Titles*, p. 43.

first instance. But in all these cases crown grants were afterwards obtained, and the colonies also passed acts with regard to the purchase of land from the natives without license from the colonies themselves, declaring all Indian deeds taken without such license to be void.*

It should be remembered, however, that the crown grant was not a grant by the English government, but solely by the King.

It has always been the theory of the English law that discovery and possession of a new country gave a valid title to its land, subject to the natural right of the natives to protection, but with no right in the natives to dispose of the land to anybody else. Under this theory the Crown was the absolute owner of the land, and could dispose of it and provide for the government of it at its discretion. For instance, grants could be made by the Crown without regard to the law of England, as was done when Charles I. authorized the grantees of land in Maryland to erect manors, anything in the statutes of *quia emptores* to the contrary notwithstanding.†

It was upon this theory of the right of the Crown, based upon the discovery by the Cabots in 1497, and the subsequent taking formal possession by Sir Humphrey Gilbert in 1583, that the land titles of the New England Colonies were founded. The crown grants of land carried with them the right to extinguish the Indian title as a matter of course, but that title was recognized as a right of occupancy. For instance, when in 1662 the town of Dedham and

---

* *Connecticut Colony Records*, Vol. I, pp. 214, 364, 402; *Massachusetts Records*, Vol. I, p. 112; *Plymouth Colony Records*, 1634.

† Hazard, *State Papers*, Vol. I, p. 335; Kent, *Commentaries*, Vol. III, p. 379 *et seq.*

some of its inhabitants had a controversy with the Indians living at Naticke as to the title of certain lands, the General Court heard the parties and declared that, though the legal right of Dedham could not be denied, yet there had been such encouragement of the Indians in their improvement of the land, as "added to their native right, which cannot in strict justice be utterly extinguished," required that the Indians be not dispossessed of the lands they were then possessed of, but that compensation be given to Dedham out of other lands not then granted.*

So in 1672, when certain inhabitants of Northampton and other towns desired a grant of land for a village at Squakeage, the land was granted upon certain conditions, and upon the further condition that, if the grantees should purchase the Indian title to the lands, it should belong to the colony, unless the grantees performed the conditions of the grant.†

In Rhode Island Roger Williams and his associates at first claimed that the only title required was the Indian title, and took conveyances of it as the titles to the land on which they settled, though they afterwards obtained and accepted a crown grant of the same land in 1663.‡

The same course was pursued in Connecticut, the lands being purchased by the first planters from the Indians, or acquired, as in the case of the Pequot territory, by conquest from the Indians. In 1662, however, the Connecticut Colony obtained a charter and a grant from the Crown.§

* *Records of Colony of Massachusetts Bay*, Shurtleff edition, Vol. IV, Part II, p. 49.

† *Ibid.*, p. 529.

‡ Arnold, *History of Rhode Island*, Vol. I, pp. 114, 284; *Rhode Island Records*, Vol. I, p. 31 *et seq.*, pp. 130, 134, 135, 143.

§ Trumbull, *History of Connecticut*, Vol. I, p. 249.

New Hampshire was created a royal province in 1680, the English Courts having held that the title was in the Crown, subject only to the vested rights of Mason in the soil, and it included, as was claimed, the territory now known as Vermont. The titles there were, from the government under the crown grants, somewhat conflicting, but all resting primarily upon the title of the Crown.*

In Plymouth the land was granted under a patent in 1620 and a royal grant in 1629.

The title to the land in Maine was granted under the Crown Charter of 1692, under the jurisdiction of Massachusetts, which had a right to grant the lands, subject to the approval of the Crown, within two years.†

[The origin of the title to land in all these colonies was, as stated at first, based upon the ownership by the Crown arising from discovery and possession, subject only to the right of the Indians, as natives of the soil, to the enjoyment of it, but with no power of disposal.

The English royal grants of the territory of the New England States began by a commission to John and Sebastian Cabot by Henry VII in A.D. 1495, authorizing them "to seek out countries or provinces of the heathen and infidels, wherever situated, hitherto unknown to all Christians, and to subdue and possess them as his subjects."‡

Under this commission the Cabots in 1497–98 landed upon the American coast, and explored it to some extent from Labrador to the Carolinas, more than a year before Columbus had seen the continent. Cabot drew charts of his voyage, which were referred to by Gilbert as existing in 1576, but have entirely dis-

---

* Belknap, *History of New Hampshire*, Vol. II, p. 205.
† *Maine Historical Collections*, Vol. I, p. 239.
‡ Hazard's *State Papers*, Vol. I, p. 9.

appeared.* Two years later a Portuguese explored Labrador. In 1507 the French visited the Gulf of St. Lawrence, and made a map of it and the neighboring country.

In 1522 there was a settlement of fishermen at Newfoundland, comprising, it is said, about fifty houses inhabited by people of different nationalities. In 1524 the French explored the coast from the Carolinas to Newfoundland, very much as the Cabots had done, but more in detail, and they called the country New France.

From 1534 to 1542 the Spaniards explored the coast of Florida, and the French erected monuments in token of possession in the region of the Gulf of St. Lawrence.

England, however, took no steps to maintain her rights as a discoverer by taking possession of the territory explored by the Cabots until 1578, when Queen Elizabeth gave a patent to Sir Humphrey Gilbert in the same terms as that given by Henry VII to the Cabots.† Gilbert landed at Newfoundland, called the merchants and masters of the ships of the various nations then there together, and took possession with prescribed legal formalities. He made laws which the people promised to obey, and made grants of land upon covenants of annual rent. Gilbert was lost at sea, but Sir Walter Raleigh, his half-brother and partner in the enterprise, obtained a similar patent in his own name, under which he was the first to occupy the soil of Virginia in 1584.‡ With his consent Gosnold visited Massachusetts Bay in 1602, but before his return to England for the purpose of obtaining supplies to establish settlements Queen Elizabeth died,

---

* Sir Humphrey Gilbert, *A Discourse of a Discouerie for a New Passage to Cataia*, London, 1576.

† Hazard, Vol. I, p. 24. ‡ Hazard, Vol. I, p. 33.

Raleigh was imprisoned, and all traces of his attempt to colonize in America disappeared.

In 1606 a patent was granted by James I, to Sir Thomas Gates and others for the Colony of Virginia, but its limits did not include the whole of the English claim to title. It extended no further south than the present boundaries of North Carolina and no further north than the present limits of the State of New Hampshire; that is, between 34° and 45° of north latitude. It provided for two colonies, one southern, between the 34th and 41st degrees, and one northern, between the 38th and 45th degrees, leaving, as may be seen, three degrees, or the territory from about the southern point of Maryland to the southern point of Connecticut, as common territory.*

In 1620 a charter was granted by James I to forty persons called "The Council established at Plymouth, in the County of Devon, for the Planting, Ruling, and Governing of New England in America." This charter referred to the patent of 1606, and granted to the persons named in it all the territory from the 40th to the 48th degrees of north latitude, and from the sea to the sea, to be called New England; that is, its territory extended from about the latitude of the city of Philadelphia to the middle of Newfoundland and from the Atlantic to the Pacific.†

The chief managers of this Council were Sir Ferdinando Gorges, Captain John Mason, and the Earl of Warwick, who was president. Gorges was to be governor of the new State. The Council made about twenty grants under their charter, but fell into difficulties, and finally came to an end in 1635.‡

---

* Hazard, Vol. I, p. 50. † Hazard, Vol. I, p. 103.

‡ A list of these grants will be found in Palfrey, Vol. I, p. 397, note, and also in "History of Grants under the Great Council for New England," by Samuel F.

March 28, 1629, a patent and charter was granted by Charles I to Sir Henry Rosewell, Sir Richard Saltonstall, John Endecott, and others, as a body corporate by the name of the "Governor and Company of the Massachusetts Bay in Newe-England."*

January 13, 1629, a grant was made by Charles I to William Bradford and his associates, reciting that they had for nine years lived in New England and "planted a towne called by the name of New-Plimouth."†

In 1630 the Council of Plymouth in the County of Devon granted to Robert, Earl of Warwick, a part of New England, including the later colony of Connecticut, and it was confirmed to him by a patent from Charles I. March 19, 1631, the Earl of Warwick granted this territory to William, Viscount Say and Seal, and ten others, and the settlers of Connecticut were granted their lands by these eleven persons, the grantees of Warwick, who was the grantee of Charles I.‡

The grants of land by the colonies under these grants from the Crown were usually made to "proprietors," who as such, or as towns, often called "plantations," granted the lands to such persons as they desired to have become inhabitants of the towns. In some cases the "proprietors" and the towns acted independently, but in most cases the "proprietors" were the town, and made grants as such.§

Haven, in *Lectures on the Early History of Massachusetts*, Lowell Institute Course. 1869. The supplement to this lecture gives an interesting chronological statement of the different charters covering the New England States.

* Hazard, Vol. I, p. 239. † Hazard, Vol. I, p. 298.

‡ Trumbull, *History of Connecticut*, Vol. I, p. 27.

§ Egleston, *Land System of New England*, p. 29.

CHAPTER II.

ADMISSION OF INHABITANTS.—GRANTS OF LAND BY TOWNS.—RESTRAINT OF ALIENATION OF LANDS.—PROCEEDINGS IN BOSTON AND OTHER MASSACHUSETTS AND PLYMOUTH TOWNS.

At first the New England towns exercised the right to exclude new-comers from inhabitancy by providing that no person should be received as an inhabitant without a vote of the town or of the "townsmen" or selectmen, and also by providing that no inhabitant should receive or entertain persons who were not admitted as inhabitants, or, as they were termed, strangers. This right of exclusion from inhabitancy was still further exercised by orders providing that inhabitants should not sell or let their land or houses to strangers without the consent of the town.

In Connecticut the colony law of 1659 provided that

> No inhabitant shall have power to make sale of his accommodation of house or lands until he have first propounded the sale thereof to the town where it is situate and they refuse to accept of the sale tendered.*

This restraint upon alienation by inhabitants of towns was not a new thing. Similar restraints existed in the Old World, and exist to-day in the village communities of Russia, where one may not sell to a stranger to the *mir*, or village, without the consent of the inhabitants.†

In addition to this right to deny admission to the town it was assumed that the right to exclude from inhabitancy included the right to admit to inhabitancy upon condition, and the towns frequently ad-

---

* *Public Records of the Colony of Connecticut*, Vol. I, p. 351.

† Egleston, *The Land System of the New England Colonies*, p. 40; Maine, *Early History of Institutions*, p. 109.

mitted inhabitants upon conditions, in some cases, that the person admitted should set up a mill within a given time and should charge only certain prices; in others, that he should practise a trade within the town; in many cases, that the person should be of "peaceable conversation" and of "inoffensive carriage"; and, in still other cases, upon security that the person admitted should not become chargeable for support to the town at any time.

The records of Boston and of other towns in the Massachusetts and Plymouth Colonies show the action of the towns.

In Boston in November, 1634, it was ordered at a general meeting that Mr. Winthrop, then also governor, and six other persons, should have the power to divide and dispose of all lands belonging to the town, not then in the lawful possession of any particular persons, to the inhabitants of the town according to the orders of the Court, leaving such portions in common for the use of new-comers and the further benefit of the town as in their discretion they should see fit. These persons were subsequently termed "Allotters."

In November, 1635, this order was passed at a general town meeting:—

It is agreed that noe further allotments shalbe graunted unto any new comers, but such as may be likely to be received members of the Congregation:

That none shall sell their houses or allotments to any new comers, but with the consent and allowance of those that are appointed Allotters.

This order against selling land to strangers was enforced. June 6, 1636, an order was made by the selectmen as follows:—

Wee finde that Richard Fairebanke hath sold unto twoe

straingers the twoe houses in Sudbury end that were William Balstones, contrary to a former order, and therefore the sayle to bee voyd, and the said Richard Fairbancke to forfeite for his breaking thereof, xls.

Wee finde that Isaacke Cullymore Carpenter hath sould his house unto a strainger, contrary to the same order, and therefore the sayle thereof to bee voyd, and the said Isaacke Cullymore to forfeite for his breaking thereof, xls.

On September 26, 1636, the records of the selectmen show that

it was founde that William Hudson hath sould an housplott and garden unto one William Mawer, a strainger, without the consent of the appointed Allotters, contrarie to a former order. xx s.

Also that William Aspewall hath sould a housplott and a garden unto one M^r. Tinge, contrarie to the same order. 2 lb.

That in like sort M^r. Samuell Cole hath sold an Allotment unto one M^r. Greenefield, and is to forfett for the breaking of the order iii lb.

On August 7, 1637, the selectmen granted leave to Richard Fairbank "to sell his shopp to —— Saunders, a booke-bynder."

On the 28th of August the record of the selectmen shows that

it is agreed that Richard Hull Carpenter shall have liberty to sell his house and ground neere John Galloppe unto Philip Sherman, of Roxbury.

In September, 1637, "Robert Gillam, marryner," was given leave "to buy a houseplott where he can."

In August, 1638, there was leave granted to Francis Lyall to become an inhabitant, and leave was "graunted to Mr. Thomas Cornnell for the buying of our brother Willyam Balstone's house, and to become an inhabitant of this Towne."

On November 2, 1638, "leave is granted to Richard Rawlings, a plasterer, to buy Peter Johnson, the Dutchman's house, and to become an Inhabitant of this Towne."

The term "townsman" seems to have been used interchangeably with that of inhabitant. November 19, 1638, the selectmen's records show that

> George Barrill, Cooper, hath for him and his heirs and assigns for £28 bought of the said Thomas Painter, his dwelling-house, with the Appurtenances, and ground Under it, in this towne, and whereto he had the Consent of the Townesmen, and soe is admitted a Townesman upon Condition of Inoffensive Carryage.
>
> [In December] one William Teffe, a Taylor, is allowed to bee an Inhabitant, and hath this day fully agreed with Jacob Wilson of his house, and the ground under it, in this towne.
>
> Also Esdras Reade, a Taylor, is this day allowed to bee an inhabitant, and to have a great Lot at Muddy River for 4 heads.

In January, 1638, appears the first record with regard to the liability of the town for the support of a person admitted into it. The record of the selectmen is as follows:—

> Richard Tuttell, our brother, hath undertaken for one Dorothie Bill, a Widowe, a Soiourner in his house to discharge the Towne of any Charge that may befall the Towne for any thing about her.

In the next month the record shows that

> Richard Wright hath sold 130 Acrs of land at Mount Woollystone to one M^r. Pane, of Concord, without the consent of the Towne's Allotters, contrary to a former Order, and he is therefore to pay for a Fyne to the towne's stocke, to be paid at the next Towne's Meeting the sume of £6.

On August 12, 1639, the record shows that

> John Seaborne, a Taylor, having served for the space of three years within this Towne, is granted to be an Inhabitant.

Also that in the next month Mr. Richard Parker, merchant, was allowed to be an inhabitant, and Mr. Thomas Foule also allowed to be an inhabitant.

The church relations of the early settlers is shown by the form of the following entries.

On November 25, 1639, the record of the selectmen shows that

> John Seaberry, a Seaman hath with leave bought our brother Water Merrye's house, and Half an Acre under it in the Mylne feild, and so is allowed for an Inhabitant.
> Also Richard Storer, the Sonne of Elizabeth Hull, the Wife of our brother Roberte Hull, is Allowed to be an Inhabitant and to have a great Lott at the Mount for three heads.
> Also our brother Arthure Perry hath leave to sell his house and garding to Silvester Saunders whoe (hath) long beene a servant in this towne.

The entries of permission or allowance to become an inhabitant occur with increasing frequency in 1639, 1640, and thereafter for a few years. One of them shows that the town regarded it as important that everybody should own his home.

On March 16, 1640, the record of the selectmen is that

> John Palmer, Carpenter, now dwelling here, is to be allowed an Inhabitant, if he can gett an house, or land to sett an house upon (it being not proper to allowe a man an Inhabitant Withou(t) habitation).

Frequently the question of whether a person should be received as an inhabitant was taken under consideration. One of the records in 1640 shows that several persons were accepted for townsmen, but that "Edw. Arnoll is taken into Consideration until the next meeting to becom a townsman."

Apparently, persons came into the town and there stayed, so that they were likely in fact to become inhabitants, although not admitted, for we find that on March 1, 1647, the following order was passed:—

> It is ordered that no Inhabitant shall entertaine man or woman from any other towne or Countrye as a sojourner or inmate with

an intent to reside here, butt shall give notice thereof to the Selectmen of the towne for their approbation within 8 dayes after their Cominge to the towne upon penalty of twenty shillings.

It is farther ordered that no Inhabitant shall farme, lett, or putt to sale to any person any howse or howses within this towne, without first acquaintinge the select men of the town theirwith.

In December, 1652, appears the first entry of the admission of a person as a townsman or inhabitant upon security. The record is:—

Att a metting of all the Seleckt men, William Gilford, Brikelayer, is admitted a Townsman. M^r. Richard Bellingham ingageth to secur the town from all dammag by Receiving of hime for one whole yeare.

At the same meeting "M^r. Pighogg, a Chururgeon, is admitted a Townsman," "John Lewes is fyned 5s. for Intertaining of Francis Burges without libertie of the seleckt men," and "Good^n Watters is fyned tenn shillings for Intertaining of Roger Sowers without libertie form the seleckt men."

On June 28, 1654, William Bruff was admitted as an "Inhabytant, William Wenbourne standing bound to the towne that he shall nott be Chargeable thereto."

[Again, February 25, 1655] Nathaneell Woodard is admitted an inhabitant, and Thomas Harwood bound in a bond of 20l. to secure the towne from any charge that may arise by the sayd Wodard or his family.

On March 31, 1656, the following record is made, which is the first record, I think, of any warning out in New England:—

Richard Pittman is fined twenty shillings for nott giving security to save the towne from charge, and to depart the towne forthwith if hee put nott in security.

Numerous entries follow of fines imposed for entertaining persons without consent of the town, of which these are illustrative:—

[March 26, 1657] George Burrill, Cooper, is fined ten shillings for intertaining Jno Gilbert into his family, withoutt consent of the towne. . . . Ralph Hutchinson is fined ten shillings for intertaining Jno. Gilbert into his family, withoutt the townes mens consent. . . . John Hart is fined ten shillings for intertaining Jno. Gilbert into his family, withoutt the townesmens consent.

On April 27, 1657, there are the following records, showing the manner in which security was given for persons admitted into the town:—

Richard Way is admitted into the Town, provided that Aron Way doe become bound in the sum of twenty pound sterll. to free the Town from any charge that may accrew to the town by the said Rich^d. or his family.

Richard Smith is admitted into the Town, being Comended to the Town by M^r. Jno. Willson, senr., provided that Henry Blague and John Pease, become bound to the Town in the sum of twenty pounds sterll.

We, William Blague and John Pease, doe heerby bind our selves, our heires, executors, &c., joyntly and severally in the full sum of twenty pound sterll. unto the select men of Boston and their successors, to secure the Town from all charge from tyme to tyme from the said Richd Smith and his family: and hereunto put our hands.

On June 29, 1657, there is the following entry, which, I think, is the first with regard to support by the town:—

It is ordered that Ensigne Jno. Web shall suply Richard Sanfurd with such necesary support as the little infant Mary Langham or the nurse thereoff either have or shall expend, untell the Town take further order.

It appears that on December 29, 1657, Richard Seward was admitted an inhabitant, Nat Fryar being bound in a bond of twenty pounds to secure the town from charge. Derman Mahoone was fined twenty

shillings for "intertaining two Irish women contrary to an order of the towne, in that case provided and is to quitt his house of them forthwith att his perill."
On January 25, 1657, it was recorded that

Elizabeth Blesdale hath liberty to reside in the towne, and William Beamsley is bound in a bond of twenty pounds to save the towne from any charge that may arise by her during her said residence, which is acknowledged by WILLIAM BEAMSLEAY.

At this time, admission as an inhabitant upon the security given by some person to save the town harmless from any charge that might afterwards arise seems to have become general, and the bond of security was ordinarily twenty pounds.*

In 1659 the entertainment of persons not admitted as inhabitants seems to have reached such an extent that a general order for the protection of the town was deemed proper, and the following order was passed June 13, 1659, at a general town meeting:—

Whereas sundry inhabitants in this towne have nott so well attended to former orders made for the securing the towne from charge by sojourners, inmates, hyred servants, journeymen, or other persons that come for help in physick or chyrurgery, whereby no litle damage hath already, and much more may accrew to the towne. For the prevention whereof Itt is therefore ordered, that whosoever of our inhabitants shall henceforth receive any such persons before named into their howses or employments without liberty granted from the select men, shall pay twenty shillings for the first weeke, and so from weeke to weeke, twenty shillings, so long as they retaine them, and shall beare all the charge that may accrew to the Towne by every such sojourner, journeyman, hired servt., Inmate, &c., received or employed as aforesaid. Provided, alwayes, that if any person so receiving any shall, within fifteene dayes, give sufficient security unto the select men that the Towne may be secured from all charges that may arise by any person received, and that the persons so received bee not of notorious evill life and manners, their fine abovesaid shall bee

* See *Boston Town Records,* 1634–1660.

remitted or abated according to the discretion of the select men. And itt is further ordered that if after bond given by any, they give such orderly notice to the select men that the towne may bee fully cleared of such person or persons so received according to law, then their bonds shall be given in againe.*

In Woburn no one was allowed to become an inhabitant without first producing evidence of his peaceable behavior, and by consent of the selectmen or the town at a public meeting. One of the original town orders provided that no person should entertain any inmate in his family, whether married or otherwise, for more than three days without the consent of four selectmen, under penalty of sixpence for the use of the town for every day.

These orders were rigorously enforced by fines for a long series of years.†

In 1648 a stranger was admitted an inhabitant of Woburn and permitted to buy land for his convenience, "provided he unsettle not any inhabitant and bring testimony of his peaceable behaviour which is not in the least measure questioned." ‡

In Scituate it was provided in 1673 that no one should have any interest in the undivided lands "that is not allowed and approved as an inhabitant of the

* See *Boston Town Records*, 1634–1660, p. 152.

This was but doing in New England what was done at the same time to some extent in England. March 13, 1664, the Steeple-Ashton vestry voted as follows:—

"Item, Whereas there hath much poverty happened unto this parish by receiving of Strangers to inhabit there and not first securing them against such contingencies, and for avoiding the like occasions in time to come,—It is ordered by this Vestry that every person who shall let or set any housing or dwelling to any Stranger, and shall not first give good security for defending and saving the said inhabitants from future charge as may happen by such Stranger coming to inhabit within the said parish, shall be rated to the poor to 20s. monthly, over and besides his monthly tax."

† Sewall, *History of Woburn*, pp. 47, 48.
‡ *Town Records of Woburn*, Vol. I, p. 13.

town of Scituate." And in 1667 the town voted that, if any person should entertain a stranger after being admonished by a committee appointed for that purpose, he should be punished by a fine of ten shillings for each week.

At the same meeting the town voted "that Mr. Black should depart the Towne presently."*

In Springfield there were very full orders in regard to the admission of inhabitants. In 1638 it was provided that no man should sell his lot to another inhabitant that had a lot, and that no man should possess two lots without the consent of the town till he had been an inhabitant five years; and that, if any man desired to sell his lot to a stranger, he might do it if the town did not "disallow of ye sd stranger," and, if it did disallow the admission of the stranger, then it should buy the lot at an appraisal within twenty days, or it should be deemed that the town allowed purchase by the stranger. This order was later changed so as to provide that no inhabitant should sell or let his land to any stranger without notifying the selectmen who the stranger was, and they allowing the admission of the stranger as an inhabitant, under penalty of twenty shillings or forfeiting the land, and, if the townsmen disallowed the admission of the purchaser, then the town might within thirty days buy the land at an appraisal, or, if they did not, then the land might be sold to the stranger who "should be esteemed as entertained or alowed of by the towne as an inhabitant."†

In 1642 the following vote was passed:—

It is agreed with the generall consent and vote of the Inhabitants of Springfield: That if any man of this Township shall under the

* Deane, *History of Scituate*, pp. 11, 110.
† Green, *History of Springfield*, pp. 48, 49.

Colour of friendship or otherwise intertayne any person or persons here, to abide or continue as inmates, or shall subdivide theyr house lots to entrtayne them as tenants or otherwise, for a longer tyme than one month, or 31 days, without the generall consent & allowance of the inhabitants (children or servants of the family that remayne single persons excepted) shall forfeit for the first default xx shillings, to be destrayned by the Constable of their goods, cattell or chattails, for ye publique use of the Inhabitants: And alsoe he shall forfeit xx shillings per month for every month that any such person or persons shall soe continue in this township, with out the generall consent of the Inhabitants: and if in ye tyme of theyr abode after ye limitation they shall neede releefe, not being able to mayntayne themselves, then he or they that entertayne such persons shall be lyable to be rated by the Inhabitants for ye releife & maintenance of the said party or parties, as the Inhabitants shall think meete.

In 1659 John Wood was called to account for giving entertainment to Isaac Hall for the space of two months, and was fined forty shillings. Quince Smith was regarded as another undesirable person, and was given liberty to tarry in town "2 months from ye 18th of December, 1660; if he tarry longer it must be by a new liberty from ye selectmen," and on the 18th of February he was warned by the selectmen to depart the town.

The sons of even the first settlers of Springfield were not admitted as inhabitants, to be voters and assume the responsibilities of citizenship, without giving bonds to the town to secure it against any charge which might possibly arise on their account. Deacon Chapin gave bonds of twenty pounds each when two of his sons were admitted, Henry in 1660 and Josiah in 1663. At the time of Henry's admission Elizur Holyoke gave bonds in the sum of twenty pounds to the town treasurer for the admission of Samuel Ely "to secure the town from any charge which may a rise to the town by the admission of the said Ely or his family."*

* Burt, *First Century of History of Springfield*, 1636–1736, Vol. I, pp. 53, 54.

In Charlestown as early as October 13, 1634, it was ordered "that none be permitted to sit down and dwell in this town without the consent of the town first obtained"; and February 21, 1637, "that no freeman should entertain any in their houses, but to give notice thereof at the next town meeting," and "none that are not free should entertain any without the consent" of three of the selectmen.

The following instances from the early records further illustrate this. In 1637 John Harvard, the founder of Harvard College, and others were admitted as inhabitants by the following order:—

"Mr. John Harvard is admitted a townsman with promise of such accommodations as we best can"; "Mr. Francis Norton is admitted a Townsman if he please"; in 1635 "Goodman Rand granted to set down with us upon condition the Town have no just ground of exception"; in 1636 "Ralph Smith was admitted a month upon trial"; in 1637 James Hoyden was admitted "if the court give way"; John Mosse, "newly out of his time," was admitted "for this year to live with his master in his family upon trial"; "Timothy Ford upon his good behaviour was admitted to plant and to be at Richard Kettle's for planting time, or to propound another place"; in 1638 "Turner was permitted for the present to sojourn with Henry Bullock till next meeting, in mean time to be enquired of."

On April 3, 1638, it was ordered that

No freeman shall entertain any person or persons at their houses, but to give notice to the Townsmen [Selectmen] within fourteen days; and such as are not free, not to entertain any at all without consent of six of the men deputed for the town affairs; and these to acquaint the town therewith at their next meeting, upon penalty of ten shillings for every month that they keep them without the town's consent; and the constable is to see this order observed from time to time, and to gather up the aforesaid fines by way of distress.*

* Frothingham, *History of Charlestown*, pp. 54, 55.

The following votes and orders are found on the records of Cambridge, then Newtowne:—

On December 5, 1636, it was

Ordered, That no man inhabiting or not inhabiting within the bounds of the town shall let or sell any house or land unto any, without the consent of the Townsmen then in place, unless it be to a member of the congregation; and lest any one shall sustain loss thereby, they shall come and proffer the same unto them, upon a day of the monthly meeting, and at such a rate as he shall not sell or let for a lesser price unto any than he offereth unto them, and to leave the same in their hands, in liking, until the next meeting day in the next month, when, if they shall not take it, paying the price within some convenient time, or provide him a chapman, he shall then be free to sell or let the same unto any other, provided the Townsmen think them fit to be received in.

Ordered, That whosoever entertains any stranger into the town, if the congregation desire it, he shall set the town free of them again within one month after warning given them, or else he shall pay 19s. 8d. unto the townsmen as a fine for his default, and as much for every month they shall there remain.*

In March, 1695,—

Voted that if any person in this Town, do Let or Tenant his house or land, within this Town to any person that is not an inhabitant in this Town, without first applying themselves to the Select men then in being for their approbation, and give in Bond to the Select men Sufficient to keep the Town from charge; if they do refuse or Neglect So to doe as above, they shall then pay a fine of fifteen shillings p month to the use of the Town for their neglect, so long as they Shall entertaine such Inhabitants or Inmates in their houses.†

On January 5, 1634, it was ordered by the town that every person to whom land was granted should either improve it or return it to the town, and, if he improved it, he should not sell it without first offering it to the town.

* Paige, *History of Cambridge, Massachusetts*, 1630–1877, p. 40.
† *Proprietors' Records of the Town of Cambridge*, 1635–1829, p. 209.

In 1636 it was ordered that

Noe man Inhabiting or not I̭habiting with in the bowndes of the towne shall lett or sell anie howse or Land vnto anie without the consent of the townsmḙ then in place vnlesse it be to a memb^r of the congregatio & least anie one shall sustaine losse therby they shall come & prffer the same vnto them vppon a daye of ye: monethly meeting & att such a Rate as he shall not sell or lett for a lesser price vnto anie than he offereth vnto them & to leave the same in there handes in lyking vntill the next Meeting daye in the next moneth when yf they shall not take it paying the pryce within some convenient tyme or prvdye him a chapman he shall then be free to sell or lett ye same vnto anie oth prvyed the townsmen think them fitt to be received in.

And it was also ordered:—

That whosoeve^r entertaynes anie p(   ) stranger into the towne yf the congregation desyr it he shall set the towne free of them againe with one moneth aft^r warnig giuen them or else he shall paye 10^s 8^d vnto the townsmen as a fyne for his default & as muche for eure moneth they shall (   ) Remaine.

In 1644

for preventing all inconveniences herein, it is Ordered by the Towsmen that no man shall Lett out his house to any person comeing from any other place to settle him or her self as an Inhabitant in o^r Towne, with out the consent of the major pr^t of the Townsmen for the time being, under the penalty of twenty shillings a weeke for eu^{r}ie such default.

In 1658 the following "proposiccon was voted by the Towne in the affirmative" in regard to the "Great Swamp lying within the bounds of this towne":—

That no person that hath any part or parcell thereof granted vnto him or shall purchase any part thereof, shall alienate the Same to any person not inhabiting wth in the bounds of this Towne, on penalty of forfeiting the Said land vnto the vse of the Towne.*

At a meeting of the selectmen in 1664,

Thomas Gleison who had been in town about a week being sent

* *Records of the Town of Cambridge*, pp. 24, 50, 125.

for to appeare before the Select men, was warned to provide Himselfe, the Townsemen not seeing meet to allow of Him as an Inhabitant in this Towne.*

The records of Salem show that nobody was permitted to become an inhabitant except by authority of the Town or the Selectmen, but land was not always allotted to persons so received. In 1636 the record shows that

> m^{rs} Keniston is recieued for Inhabitant but not to haue land but what she purchaseth, & so hath purchased Lieft: Dauenports house.

In February, 1636, Debora Holmes was refused an allotment of land because she was a maid, and it "would be a bad president to keep hous alone." As a solace for this rejection, however, it appears that she was given four bushels of corn.

On the 23d of the same month various persons were received for inhabitants, one without grants of land and one "to purchase his accomodacōn." Similar entries were very frequent during 1636 and 1637 and the following years of the early settlement of the town.†

In Dedham the town covenant signed by the first settlers, 126 in number, in 1636 provided as follows:—

> We engage by all means to keep off from our company such as shall be contrary-minded, and receive only such into our society as will in a meek and quiet spirit promote its temporal and spiritual good.

The first by-law adopted provided that a committee should be appointed to examine the character of newcomers, and make report of their inquiries to the town, and that all persons coming into the town should

---

* *Town Records of Cambridge*, p. 155.

† *Town Records of Salem*, 1634–1659 (William P. Upham, Essex Institute Historical Collections), pp. 32, 35.

declare their names and explain their motives, and that servants should bring testimony of good character before being permitted to abide in the town.*

In Watertown it was voted that "no foreigner of England or some other plantation shall have liberty to sit down amongst us, unless he first have the consent of the freemen of the town."†

In 1680 an inhabitant was brought before the selectmen to answer for entertaining one of his sisters who was newly married, and required to give a bond for forty pounds in behalf of his sister and her husband that they should not become chargeable to the town.‡

In 1644 it was ordered by the townsmen of Cambridge that

no person with his family shall come as an Inhabitant in to o^r Towne, with out the consent of the major part of the Townsmen for the time being, under the penalty of 20^s. for eu^{r}ie weeke.§

In Lancaster it was ordered that "for the better preserving of the puritie Religion and ourselves from the infection of Error not to distribute allotments and to receive into the plantation as inhabitants any excommunicate or otherwise profane and scandalous (known so to be) nor any notoriously erring against the doctrine and discipline of the churches and the State and Government of this Commonweale."||

In Groton, June 2, 1669, we find the record to be that "the towne did solemlie determine to take in no more but a taylear and a smith," and later that "it was the towne's mind" that "onely a smith and no other" could be admitted.**

* Worthington, *History of Dedham*, pp. 32, 33.
† Bond, *History and Genealogy of Watertown*, p. 995.
‡ MacLear, *Early New England Towns*, Columbia University Studies, Vol. XXIX, No. 1, p. 134.
§ *Cambridge Town Records*, p. 50. || *Early Records of Lancaster*, p. 28.
** Green, *Early Records of Groton*, pp. 25, 26.

In Braintree, Massachusetts, it was ordered in 1641, that no inhabitant should sell or dispose of any house or land "to any one that is not received an inhabitant into the town" without it was first offered to the selectmen, and, in case it was not bought by them within twenty days, then it might be sold, but only "to such as the townsmen shall approve."

In March, 1681, it was ordered that no inhabitant should entertain any stranger without leave from the selectmen upon penalty of ten shillings for every three days of such entertainment.*

In Weymouth in 1646 a vote was passed forbidding any inhabitant from receiving as an inmate any stranger without giving the town an indemnity bond against damage under a penalty of a fine of five shillings per week; and no inhabitant could sell or let to any stranger either house or land without having first tendered the same to the town at a training, lecture, or other public meeting.†

The early settlers of Medfield in 1650 signed an agreement, the preamble to which is interesting:—

> Forasmuch as for the further promulgation of the Gospell the subdueing of this pt of the earth amongst the races given to the sonns of Adam & the enlargmt of the bounds of the habitations formerly designed by God to som of his people in this wilderness it hath pleased the Lord to move and direct [etc.].

The third article of the agreement was that

> We shall all of us in the said Towne Faithfully endeavour tht onely such be receaved to our societie & Township as we may have sufficient satisfaction in, that they ar honest, peacable, & free from scandall and eronious opinnions.

In Saco it was voted by the townsmen, September 27, 1653, that Roger Spencer and "his heirs forever"

---

* Bates, *Braintree Town Records*, pp. 2, 20.
† Nash, *History of Weymouth*, p. 32.

should have liberty to set up a saw-mill, provided he did so within a year, and on condition that all townsmen should have boards twelvepence in a hundred cheaper than any stranger, and also that townsmen should be employed in the mill before a stranger, "provided they doo their worke so cheap as a stranger."

In a similar grant in January, 1654, to one John Davis, it was a condition of the grant that he should employ townsmen before others, strangers, and buy provisions of townsmen before strangers at price current, and that the town was to have boards for their own use at tenpence a hundred under current price.

In 1654 it was ordered "that if any outner desire to come into towne to inhabite they shall put in sufisient security not to be chargeable to the towne."*

In Billerica, in November, 1654, the town adopted

Sertin Orders made by vs the present inhabitantes of the Towne of Billericey, for ye weall of y^e [town]:

1^{ly}. [That wh]at person or persons soever [shall] propound themselves to be [inhabi]tantes amongste vs, to p^{r}take of [the pr]iviledges of the comons, devitions [of la]ndes, &c., if not known to vs, he or they shall bring with them a certificate from the place from whence they come, such a testimony as shall be satisfactory to o^r towne, or select p^{r}sons of the same, before they shall be admitted as inhabitants amongste vs, to p^{r}take of any priviledges as aforesaid with vs; and after their Admission they shall subscribe their names to all the orders of the Towne, with o^{r}selves, y^t are or shall be made for the public good of the place, as also for baring vp their proportions in all publique charges, in Church, Towne, or comon weall, with those persons that came vp at the first, and so shall have their priviledges in equall proportion.†

In Chelmsford an order was passed as early as 1656 that no person should own land until he had been approved and admitted as an inhabitant by a majority

* Folsom, *History of Saco and Biddeford*, pp. 99, 100.
† Hazen, *History of Billerica, Massachusetts*, p. 53.

vote at a public town meeting. In the same year an inhabitant was admitted and granted land, "provided he set up his trade of weaving and perform the town's work." Another inhabitant was admitted and given a grant of land, "provided he set up a saw-mill and supply the town with boards at three shillings a hundred, or saw one log for the providing and bringing of another." This inhabitant, Samuel Adams, was also granted other land in consideration of his putting up a corn-mill, and the town passed an order "that no other corn-mill shall be erected for this town, provided the said Adams keep a sufficient mill and miller."*

In 1657 the selectmen of Salem cautioned the inhabitants of that town to comply with the colony ordinance of 1637 with regard to admitting inhabitants, upon a penalty of twenty shillings a week during its violation.

In 1660 two persons were fined in Salem for entertaining a stranger. In 1669 two persons were fined twenty shillings apiece for entertaining a Quaker, who was warned to depart, but persevered and subsequently became an inhabitant. In 1670 a person was appointed and instructed

to goe from house to house aboute the towne, once a moneth, to inquire what strangers are come, or haue priuily thrust themselues into towne and to giue notice to the Selectmen in beinge, from tyme to tyme, and he shall haue the fines for his paynes or such reasonable satisfaction as is meet.

In Rowley, in 1660, it was ordered:—

That no land be sold or granted by the Town unless twice published to the Town in open meeting on different days previous to the day the grant is made. The consent of adjoining owners is also required. The towns are not to exchange any land but in the same way. No tenant is to be taken into any house but by

* Allen, *History of Chelmsford*, pp. 17, 18.

Warning Out in New England 37

consent of the Town on penalty of 19 shillings per month. No man is to sell house or land to a stranger without first offering it to the Selectmen to be appraised by indifferent men on penalty of 19 shillings per month for each parcel.*

In Hadley it was voted, October 8, 1660, that no person should be owned for an inhabitant or have liberty to vote or act in town affairs until he should be legally received as an inhabitant.†

In Andover in 1660 persons were prohibited to build upon any house lots not granted to them for that purpose upon a penalty of twenty shillings a month, the records stating that "the town having given houselots to build on to all such as they have received as inhabitants of the town."‡

In 1661 it was ordered by the town of Sandwich that two persons

> have power to take notice of such as intrude themselves into the town without the town's consent and prevent their residing here.§

On December 3, 1668, the town of Plymouth voted that

> The Celect men shall hensforth have full power to Require any that shall Receive any stranger soe as to entertaine them into theire house to give Cecuritie unto them to save the Towne harmles from any damage that may acrew unto them by theire entertainment of such as aforsaid,

and also voted that "John Everson be forthwith warned to depart the towne with all Convenient speed."

On August 22, 1681, the town passed an order that

> Noe houskeeper or other in this Towne Resideing in the Towne shall entertaine any stranger into theire houses above a fortnight without giveing Information to the Celect men or some one

---

* Gage, *History of Rowley*, p. 140.
† Judd, *History of Hadley*, p. 23.
‡ Abbott, *History of Andover*, p. 48.
§ Freeman, *History of Cape Cod*, Vol. II, p. 266.

of them therof upon the forfeiture of ten shillings a weeke for all such time as any such stranger shalbe soe entertained and stay without the said Information: To be levied on the estate of such house keepers or others that shall neglect to Informe as aforsaid:

And incase the Celect men upon Information as aforsaid shall see cause to either take bonds for every such stranger either; to keep and save the Towne harmles from any damage that may acrew unto the Towne by the stay of such stranger or strangers in the Towne or expell them out of the Towne; the Celect men are heerby Impowered to doe either as they shall see Reason and cause.*

In Middleboro inhabitants were admitted by a vote of the town. One record, June 11, 1695, reads,—

"The town jointly agreed together by their vote to accept of certain" persons named "as townsmen and to have the privileges of the same."†

In Roxbury in 1672 it was ordered that no new person should be admitted to any family for more than one week without permission from the selectmen under a penalty of twenty shillings.‡

The division of lands to inhabitants, the restraint upon alienation of lands, admission of inhabitants and warning out of persons not admitted, are well illustrated in the conduct of the early settlers of Dorchester. The settlers of this town agreed on October 8, 1633, to meet once a month at eight o'clock in the morning, and

presently upon the beating of the drum, at the meeting house, there to settle such orders as may tend to the general good.

In November of the same year they ordered that such as desired to have lots should manifest the same upon the monthly meetings, that then the inhabitants present might act upon the same, and, if they

---

* *Records of the Town of Plymouth*, Vol. I, pp. 106, 169.
† Weston, *History of Middleboro*, p. 561.
‡ *Roxbury Town Records*, p. 72.

Warning Out in New England 39

approved, decide where the lands were to be given in the town. In the next year on November 3 they ordered

that no man within the Plantation shall sell his house or lott to any man without the Plantation whome they shall dislike off.

In December, 1658, the town took action as follows:

Whereas the generall Court hath taken care what strangers shall Reside in this iurisdiction and how lisenced as by the law title strangers it doth appeare, but haue taken noe order for families ore p'sons that remoue from one towne in this Jurisdiction to an other: now to p'vent such inconvenience as may come if euery one be at liberty to receive into this towne whom they please. It is ordered therfore by the select men of this towne that if any maner of p'son ore p'sons in this towne shall intertaine any soiornour ore inmate into his or ther house ore habitation aboue one weeke without lisence from the selectmen ore the maior parte of them first had and obtained, shall forfeit five shillings, and for every weekes continuance three shillings foure pence. And if any p'son as afore sayd shall receiue any family into his or ther house ore habitation longer then the time aboue sayd shall forfeit the penaltie of twenty shillings, and for euery weekes continuance 13^s: 4^d: all which fines shall be forth with taken by distresse ore otherways by warent from the select men from time to time.

On December 9, 1664, we find this order:—

This same day Clement Maxfild, appeared before the select men, and desired that his Brother John Maxfild, being arrived lately from England, might continue in the Towne with him; and that he would secure the Towne, from any dammage, during his residence here, which was granted that he, the sayd Clement Maxfild, might, entertaine his brother as is aboue expressed, vntill such time, as his Brother, shall otherwise settle himself heere, or elswhere.

The Selectmen of Dorchester doe accept of the Request of the Selectmen of Boston on the behalfe of the widow Collins, and doe grant her liberty to remaine, and reside here amongst us, till the 1. day of May, 1666.

On December 12, 1665, the record shows the following:—

There was presented vnto the Selectmen of Dorchester a note from the Select men of Boston, containing a Request from them, that the Widow Collins might be permitted by us to passe the winter here in our Towne and thereby engaging themselues, that her reception should not disoblige them from the duty they owe her, as one of their Inhabitants.

In 1667

Frances Oliuer came to the Select men and desiered liberty to be an inhabetant in this towne but he refusing to secuer the towne from damedge was not admitted.

In 1667 there is the following order:—

Richard Curtice came to the Select men, and desiered ther app'bation to Come into the Towne to liue, which was granted on Condition that he doe make ouer his house and land at Melton for the Towns Security that he be not chargable to the towne.

And

the same day William Sumner was desiered to speak with the Widdow Hims (who is lately come into this towne) to informe her that she must returne to the place from whence she came.

In April, 1668, Ralph Bradice was admitted as an inhabitant upon the agreement of John Gornell, in whose house he was, that he would be bound to secure the town from any damage therefrom. In the same year we find that

Frances Oliuer Came againe and desiered liberty to stay in the Towne and for that end brought Thomas Bird and Joseph Long to be bound for him but they vnderstanding that they must be bound to Cleere him wholly from the Towne for three months after he was remoued, refused soe to doe and therfore the said Oliuer was againe warned to depart the Town.

Family relations had no effect upon this conduct of the town with regard to inhabitancy. On November 13, 1669, the record shows that it was agreed that ther should be an order sent to John pope (the Select men vnder standing that a daughter of his is to come from Boston into his famely) that he doe forthwith come to the Select men and giue Securety to saue the Towne harmles from Damedg or els to expect the penalty which the towne order lays vpon such as entertaine Inmats.

In January, 1670, it appears that notice was given to Henery Merrifeild

to discharge the towne of his daughter Funnell which hath been at his hous about a weeke; vnless he gitt a note vnder the hands of the Select men of Melton that they will receaue her againe if need be and to looke at her as an Inhabetant of their Towne, notwithstanding her residence at her fathers hous for the p^{r}sent.

On November 14, 1670, Timothy Tilston gave bond to the selectmen to save the town harmless from any damage and charges that might arise by reason of James Bridgman, his father-in-law, "Inhabiting in Dorchester or any of his while he or they remaine in Dorchester."

In 1671

Frances Bale was called before the Select men, and his fine demanded for Entertaining his Brother in law phillip Searle and his famely in his house without licence from the Select men, whose answer was that he was speedyly to remoue his dwelling to Rocksbery.

The same day a warrant was Isued out to Constable Tilstone to giue notice vnto Henery Roberts for to depart the towne, who is now abiding at danil Ellens.

The same day petter Lyon being caled before the Select men, and at that time desiered liberty for to entertaine peter Greene of Concord into his famely for one month which was granted him, p'uided he Cleer the towne of him at that time.

On November 4, 1671, the record shows that a warrant was directed

to the Constable for to goe vp to Capt. Claps farme wher Henery Merrifeild doe lieue and to enquier whether his daughter which marryed funnell be abiding at his hous, which if she be, then to demand or take by distress ten shillings for his entertaining her Contrary vnto the towne order.

On the eighth day of the next month

the wife of Henery Merrifeild appeared before the Select men, to answer for entertaining of their daughter Funnell, Contrary to towne order, whose answer was, that she was their daughter and Could not turn her out of doars this winter time but she would willingly returne to her husband as soone as a passadg p^rsents; but they weer not approued in entertaining her, but the penalty of the town order the Select men would remitt and would leaue it to the County Court to determine the thing, if in Casse she be not gon before.

In 1672 there is the following record:—

The Select men haueing sent for John plum and his daughter Mercy, and finding that his said daughter being marryed to Thomas Chub of Beuerlee, and being alsoe neere the time of her deliuery is not p'uided for by her said husband, nor taken home to him, but continues heer with her father, contrary to good order, and to the hazarding of a charge vpon the towne, doe therfore order and requier, that the said Mercy Chub doe speedily within Six or eight days leaue this towne, and betake herself to her said husband. And doe also warne and order the said John Plum that he noe longer entertaine his said daughter, but hasten her to her husband as aforesaid vpon the penalty by the Town order in that Case p'uided, and of being complained of further to Authorety that soe the towne may be saued harmeless.

In 1673

John plum was called before the Select men to giue an accompt of his entertaining his Sonne Chub and his wife, whose answer was that his Sonne in law was gon and the Select men ordered him to discharge the towne of his daughter alsoe, forthwith.

In November, 1677, the records show that

Doctor Snellen of Boston Came to the Select men to obtaine libertie for to bring his wife and famely into this towne because of the pox increasing in Boston which libertie was granted him for two months but if he stayed longer to giue bond to secure the towne.

In 1678 one John Brown was warned out of town, and appeared before the selectmen and said he

thought that he might Come into town to be inhabetant becaus born in the town and that he might be an help to his father and mother, the Select men did Respit the full determination at that time to know the towns mind therin and in the meane time his warning out of towne to continue in force.

On the ninth day of December, 1679, the record shows that

a warrant was sent to the Constables to take a fine of John Jackson for fower weeks entertainement of Op'tunetie Lane Lane his daughter in law Contrary to towne order, and also to warne the said Opertunitie to dep^t the towne or giue in securitie to secur the towne from damedg and also that if the said Jackson entertaine her longer he must expect to pay 3^s. 4^d. p weeke for euery weeke after the date heerof: Shortly after the said Jackson came and he and William Cheney entered into 30^{ls} bond to secuer the towne. the bond is on file.

In 1681 the record shows that one Joseph Weeks

Came to the Select men and desiered libertie to take a nurst Child of one Mr Steuens of Boston, Answer was returned that though the man may be sufficcient, yet becaus it may not be a p^{r}sedent vnto others he was ordered to appoint the man to giue something vnder his hand to some one of the Select men to secure the towne.

In April, 1682, the record shows that it was

agreed by the select men that a warrant should be sent to the Constable to require a penalty according to the towne order of those that did entertaine inmates without giueing bonds for the townes security.

In Duxbury it was voted May 16, 1774, that the treasurer should prosecute all persons that might take in any persons or families belonging to any other town "as tenants, or servants, or friendship, or any straggling persons whatsoever into their houses or shelters," without giving the selectmen written notice of the names of such persons, and the places from whence they last came, within twenty days after they took them in.*

In Plymouth none could come to inhabit without leave, and, if he did, was to be warned to go away under a penalty of five shillings a week.

Inhabitants were forbidden to sell or to let houses or lands to persons not admitted as inhabitants. And no one was allowed to depart from his own town without leave of the governor and two magistrates under penalty of forfeiting all his personal property.†

For instance, in one case it was ordered as follows:

> Whereas Mr. Thacher, Mr. Crowe, & Mr. Howes, the committees of Yarmouth, were complayned of to haue made vnequall diusions of lands there, wherevpon the said comittees haue exhibited a very formall diusion of the said lands vnto the Court, wch is well approoued of, and the Court doth further order, that the said comittees shall receiue no more inhabitante into the said towne, except they bring certificate from the places whence they come, vnder sufficient mens hande of the s̃d place, of their religious and honest carriage, wch certifycate shall first be allowed by the goûn^r and assistante before such psons be admitted there.‡

The following order from the records of the town of Plymouth is a sample of their orders with regard to strangers:—

> It is enacted by the Towne that noe houskeeper or other in this Towne Resideing in the Towne shall entertaine any stranger into theire houses above a fortnight without giveing Information to the Celect men or some one of them thereof upon the forfeiture of ten shillings a weeke for all such time as any such stranger shalbe

---

* Winsor, *History of Duxbury*, p. 87.
† Freeman, *History of Cape Cod*, Vol. I, pp. 297, 298.
‡ *Plymouth Colony Records*, Vol. I (1633–1640), p. 142.

Warning Out in New England 45

soe entertained and stay without the said Information: To be levied on the estate of such house keepers or others that shall neglect to Informe as aforsaid:

And incase the Celect men upon Information as aforsaid shall see cause to either take bonds for every such stranger either; to keep and save the Towne harmles from any damage that may acrew unto the Towne by the stay of such stranger or strangers in the Towne or expell them out of the Towne; The Celect men are heerby Impowered to doe either as they shall see Reason and cause.*

To the Constables of the Town of Plimouth in the County of Plymouth, or Either of them Greeting.

These are in his Majesty's Name to Will and Require you Forthwith To Warn & Give Notice to Zepheniah Doten and his Familly Who Came Into this Town the latter End of April Last or the beginning of May, From the Town of Plimton That They Immediately Depart This Town or else they may expect to be proceeded Against According to Law, Also you are Alike Required to Warn & Give Notice to Reginald Mackreth a Stranger Who came From Liverpool In Nova Scotia into this Town in the Month of October Last that he Depart This Town Immediately or that otherwise be will be preceeded against according to Law. And you are alike Required to Warn & Give Notice to Abigail Waite Who came into this Town in the month of February Last from the Town of Hardwick In the County of Worcester that she Depart This Town Immediately otherwise She may Expect to be proceeded Against according to Law. Hereof fail Not and make Return of this Warrant and your Doings Therein To the Selectmen of Plymouth as Soon as May be.

Plymouth April ye 11, 1764.†

* *Records of the Town of Plymouth*, 1636–1705, Vol. I, p. 169.
† *Ibid.*, 1743–1783, Vol. III, pp. 152, 153.

CHAPTER III.

Massachusetts Colony and State Laws.—Plymouth Colony Laws.—Further Illustrations of Town Action as to Inhabitancy, Alienation of Land, Warning Out, etc.

These proceedings of the Massachusetts and Plymouth towns with regard to inhabitancy of newcomers were not only regarded as within the power of towns, as such, independent of any colony statute or order, but were recognized and required by colony laws prior to 1692.

May 17, 1637, the General Court of the Massachusetts Colony passed the following order:—

It is ordered, that no towne or pson shall receive any stranger, resorting hither wth intent to reside in this iurisdiction, nor shall alow any lot or habitation to any, or intertaine any such above three weekes, except such pson shall have alowance vnder the hands of some one of the counsell, or of two other of the magistrates, vpon paine that $ev^{r}y$ towne that shall give or sell any lot or habitation to any such, not so alowed, shall forfet 100s for every offence, & $ev^{r}y$ pson receiving any such, for longer time than is heare expressed, (or then shalbe alowed in some speciall cases, as before, or in case of intertainement of freinds resorting from some other parts of this country for a convenient time,) shall forfet for $ev^{r}y$ offence 40s; and for $ev^{r}y$ month after such pson shall there continew 20s; provided, that if any inhabitant shall not consent to the intertainment of any such person, & shall give notice thereof to any of the magistrates w^{th}in one month after, such inhabitant shall not bee lyable to any part of this penulty.*

In 1638 it was provided by the General Court that the constables of the several towns

should informe of newe comers, if any bee admitted w^{th}out license; & to that end warrant to bee sent out to the cunstable

* *Massachusetts Colony Records*, Vol. I, pp. 196, 241.

of each towne, to informe the Court of Assistants, wch is to consider of the fines, whether to take them or to mitigate them.

In June, 1650, another law to prevent strangers coming into the colony was passed as follows:—

Whereas wee are credibly informed that great mischeifes and outrages have binn wrought in other plantacõns in America by comãnders, and souldjers of seuerall qualitjes, and other straingers issuing out of other parts, vsurping power of goũnement ouer them, plundering of their estates, taking vp armes, and making great divisions amongst the inhabitants where they have come, to prevent the like mischeife in this jurisdiccõn, this Court doth order, and it is heereby enacted, that henceforward all straingers, of what qualitje soeuer, above the age of sixteene yeeres, ariving heere in any portes or parts of this jurisdiccõn in any shipp or vessell, shall imediately be brought before the Goũno^r, Dep^t Goũno^r, or two other magistrates, by the master or mate of the sajd shipps or vessells, vpon the poenalty of twenty pounds; for default thereof, there to give an accompt of their occasions and busines in this countrje, whereby satisfaccõn may-be given to this comõnwealth, and order taken wth such straingers as the sajd Goũn^r, Depu^t Goũno^r, two Assistants, or the next Countje Court shall see meete; and that the lawe for intertajning of straingers be strictly putt in execution, and this order to be posted vp vpon the seuerall meetinghouses doores, or postes, or other publicke places in the port tounes of this jurisdiccõn. And it is ordered, that the capt̃ of the Castle shall make knoune this order to euery shippe or vessell as it passeth by, and the constables of euery port toune shall indeavor to doe the like to such shipps or vessels before they land their passengers; and that a true record be kept of all the names of such straingers, and their qualities, by the clarks of the writts, who shall have the names given them by the sajd Goũn^r or Magistrates, to be retourned to the next jmediate sessions of the Generall Court. This to continew and be in force till the next session.*

It is said that this order, although general in its terms, was passed specially with reference to the fact that it was known that many of the friends of Wheel-

* *Records of Massachusetts Bay*, 1650, 22 June (20), pp. 23, 24.

wright and persons who entertained the Antinomian heresy were about to arrive upon a ship from England.*

But in October, 1651, another order, continuing it in force without limit of time, was made, as follows:—

Whereas there was a law made in the yeere 1650, concerning straungers coming into this jurisdictjon, wherein all straungers ariving within any of our port tounes, above the age of sixteene yeres, were enjoyned to be accomptable before the Gouernor, Dep^t Gouernor, or two of the honnored magistrates of the occasion of their coming into these parts, as in that order more largely doth appeare, which sajd order is long since expired, itt is therefore heereby ordered, that the sajd lawe be againe revived, and declared by this Courte to stand in force till this Court shall see just cawse to repeale the same.†

In 1655 complaint was made to the General Court that strangers came into town without the consent of the inhabitants, and caused charges to the town for their support, and an order was passed providing that persons who should be brought into the town without the consent of the "prudential men"—that is, the selectmen—should not be chargeable for their support to the town, but to those who were the cause of their coming in, as follows:—

All townes in this jurisdiction shall haue libertie to p̂vent the coming in of such as come from other parts or places of theise jurisdictions, & that all such psons as shalbe brought into any such towne without the consent & allowance of the prudentiall men, shall not be chargeable to the townes where they dwell, but, if necessitie require, shalbe releiued & mayntayned by those that were the cause of their coming in, of whom ye towne or select men are hereby empowred to require securitie at their entrance, or else forbid them entertaynment.‡

* *Winthrop*, Vol. I, p. 267.
† *Records of Massachusetts Bay*, Vol. IV, Part I, p. 63.
‡ *Ibid.*, p. 230.

In May, 1659, the following order was passed:—

For the avoyding of all future inconvenjencjes referring to the setling of poore people that may neede releife from the place where they dwell, itt is ordered by this Court and the authoritje thereof, that where any person, wth his family, or in case he hath no family, shall be resident in any toune or peculjar* of this jurisdiccõn for more then three moneths wthout notice given to such person or persons by the constable, or one of the selectmen of the sajd place, or theire order, that the toune is not willing that they should remajne as an inhabitant amongst them, and in case, after such notice given, such person or persons shall, notwthstanding remajne in the sajd place, if the selectmen of the sajd place shall not, by way of complaint, petition the next County Court of that shiere for releife in the sajd case, & the same prosecuted to effect, euery such person or persons (as the case may require) shall be provided for & releived, in case of necessity, by the inhabitants of the sajd place where he or she is so found.†

When the Massachusetts, Plymouth, and Connecticut Colonies confederated under Articles of Confederation for mutual defence in 1672, the right of towns to warn strangers to depart was expressly recognized by Article 13 of the Articles of Confederation, as follows:—

13. It is alsoe agreed for settleing of vagabonds and wandering persons remoueing from one Collonie to another to the disatisfaction and burthen of the places where they come as dayly experience sheweth vs; for the future it is ordered, "that wher any person or persons shalbe found in any Jurisdiction to haue had theire abode for more than three monthes and not warned out by the authoritie of the place; and incase of the neglect of any person soe warned as abouesaid to depart; if hee be not by the first oppertunitie that the season will permitt sent away from Constable to Constable; to the end that hee may be returned to the place of his former aboad; euery such person or persons shalbe

---

* A "peculiar" is a village or a new settlement within the territory of a town, as Muddy River (Brookline).
In English law a parish which has jurisdiction of ecclesiastical matters.

† *Records of Massachusetts Bay*, Vol. IV, Part I, p. 365.

accoumpted an Inhabitant where they are soe found, and by them gouerned and provided for as theire condition may require and in all such cases the Charge of the Constables to be bourne by the Treasurer where the said Constables doe dwell.*

This order, it will be observed, recognizes the right of the towns to notify persons coming into the place that they are not willing the persons should remain as inhabitants; that is, to warn them out of the town. In 1675 the Indian wars forced many people to leave their homes and go to other places, and, to prevent such persons from becoming chargeable to the towns into which they were obliged to go, the General Court passed an order providing that such persons should not, by virtue of their residence in the towns to which they went, become inhabitants thereof, or the towns become chargeable for their support, as follows:—

This court considering the inconvenience and damage which may arise to particular towns by such as, being forced from their habitations through the present calamity of the war, do repair unto them for succour: Do order and declare, that such persons, being inhabitants of this jurisdiction, who are so forced from their habitations and repair to other plantations for relief, shall not by virtue of their residence in said plantations they repair unto be accounted or reputed inhabitants thereof, or imposed upon them according to law, tit. Poor, but in such case, and where necessity requires, by reason of inability of relations &c. they shall be supplied out of the publick treasury; and that the selectmen of each town inspect this matter, and do likewise provide that such men or women may be so employed and children disposed of, that as much as may be publick charge may be avoided.   (July, 1675.)†

This order recognized colony poor to be supported at the general public charge.

* "Articles of Confederation between the Plantations under the Gouerment of the Massachusetts; The Plantations under the Gouernment of New Plymouth; and the Plantations under the Gouerment of Conecticott; Article 13. September the fift, 1672." Hazard, Vol. II, p. 525.

† *Massachusetts Colony Ancient Laws and Charters*, Chap. LXXV.

The increase of population and the desire of persons to move from one place to another in the colony, however, began to make it practically impossible to enforce the right of towns to exclude new-comers from inhabitancy by physically preventing them from coming in, or removing them, if they did come into the town. New persons came into the different towns and resided therein, and they were entertained, notwithstanding the laws against it, so that the towns became liable to the support of persons whom they did not actually admit by vote of the inhabitants or action of the town authorities.

In this state of affairs, relief was given to the towns by legislation, authorizing them to warn new-comers to depart from the towns, and providing that, if they were so warned, their subsequent living in the town should not make them inhabitants entitled to support in case of poverty.

In November, 1692, an act was passed specially providing for warning persons who might come into a town to leave it, and for a record of the names of such persons, and a warning to them in court, as follows:—

If any person or persons come to sojourn or dwell in any town and be there received and entertained by the space of three months, not having been warned by the constable, or other person whom the selectmen shall appoint for that purpose, to leave the place, and the names of such persons with the time of their abode there and when such warning was given them returned into Court of quarter sessions, every such person shall be deemed an inhabitant of such town and the proper charge of the same in case through sickness, lameness, or otherwise, they come to stand in need of relief to be borne by such town. Unless relatives be of sufficient ability to do so &c.*

* *Massachusetts Province Laws*, State edition, Vol. I, p. 67.

March 14, 1700, a further act was passed with regard to the admission of inhabitants into towns, which recognized the method of warning out as well established. Section 5 of that Act provided that no town shall "be chargeable with the support of any person residing therein who has not been approved as an inhabitant by the town or the selectmen" as in the Act provided, unless they had "continued their residence there by the space of twelve months next before and *not been warned* in manner as the law directs to depart and leave the town, any law, usage or custom to the contrary notwithstanding."

Section 6 provided that if any person not an inhabitant, "orderly warned to depart" and sent by warrant of a justice of the peace to the town where he properly belonged or to the place of his last abode, should come back to the town from which he had been warned and sent, he should be proceeded against as a vagabond.*

January 5, 1739, an Act was passed declaring the meaning of the Act of 1700, and that no taxing of any person not admitted as an inhabitant by the town or the selectmen should make the town chargeable for the support of that person, and that no forbearance of the selectmen to "warn the person to depart the town" should relieve the person by whom such person was received from the charge of his support, etc.†

February 11, 1793, an Act was passed repealing all laws as to town settlements and providing how settlements should be thereafter gained,‡ and with this went all provisions for warning out of town, and no such warning has since existed in Massachusetts.

---

* *Massachusetts Province Laws*, State edition, Vol. I, p. 453.
† *Ibid.*, p. 995.
‡ *Laws and Resolves of Massachusetts*, 1793, Chap. 34.

Warning Out in New England 53

It is interesting to note, however, that the original theory of inhabitancy by consent of the town was preserved in this statute. Among the eight different methods by which it was provided that legal settlements could be obtained was this:—

Any person that shall be admitted an inhabitant by any town or district at any legal meeting, in the warrant for which an article shall be inserted for that purpose, shall thereby gain a legal settlement therein.

This provision was retained in the law of the Commonwealth in the revision of the statutes in 1836,* and in the revision in 1860,† and only disappeared in the revision of 1882.

The Act of 1793 also had another provision that

All settled, ordained Ministers of the Gospel shall be deemed as legally settled in the towns or districts wherein they are or may be settled and ordained.

This provision has been continued until the present time, and now exists as follows:—

A settled, ordained minister of the gospel shall acquire a settlement in the place wherein he is settled.‡

In the Colony of New Plymouth it was enacted in 1636

That noe person or persons hereafter shall be admitted to live and inhabite within the Government of New Plymouth without the leave and likeinge of the Governour or two of the Assistants at least.

In 1658 another order was passed reciting the order of 1636, as follows:—

Whereas it hath bine an ancient and wholesome order bearing date March the seventh 1636 that noe pson coming from other

---

* *Revised Statutes*, Chap. 45, Sect. 1.

† *General Statutes*, Chap. 69, Sect. 1.

‡ *Revised Laws of Massachusetts*, Chap. 80, Sect. 1.

ptes bee alowed an Inhabitant of this Jurisdiction but by the approbacon of the Govr and two of the Majistrates att least and that many persons contrary to this order of Court are crept into some townshipes of this Jurisdiction which are and may bee a great desturbance of our more peacable proceedings, bee it enacted by the Court and the authoritie thereof that if any such pson or psons shalbee found that hath not doth not or will not apply and approve themselves soe as to procure the approbacon of the Govr and two of the Assistants that such bee inquired after, and if any such psons shalbee found that either they depart the Gov^rment or else that the Court take some such course therin as shalbee thought meet.*

In the compilation of Plymouth Laws in 1671, it was provided

That no person shall come into any Town or Peculiar in this Government to live and inhabitant, without the leave and approbation of the Governour and two of the Assistants at the least.

It was then provided that "every Town in this Government shall maintain their own poor," and also

That if any person come to live in any Town in this Government, and be there received and entertained three months, if by sickness, lameness or the like, he comes to want relief, he shall be provided for by that Town wherein he was so long entertained, and shall be reputed their proper charge, unless such person have within the said three months been warned by the Constable, or some one or more of the Select men of that Town, not there to abide without leave first obtained of the Town, and certifie the same to the next Court of Assistants, who shall otherwise order the person or charge arising about him, according to justice.

But if any children or elder persons shall be sent, or come from one Town to another, to be nursed, schooled, or otherwise Educated, or to a Physitian or Chyrurgeon to be cured of any disease or wound, &c. if such come to stand in need of relief, they shall be relieved and maintained by the Township whence they came, and not by that Township where they are so nursed, educated or at cure; And in case they come or be sent from any place out of this Colony; then if the Nurse, Educator, Physi-

* *Compact, Charter and Laws of Colony of New Plymouth*, pp. 57, 119.

tion or Chyrurgeon do not take good security to discharge the Town wherein he lives from all cost and charge, which shall or may befal concerning them, he that so received them shall be the Towns security in their behalf.*

Warning out was practised generally by the Massachusetts and Plymouth towns under this legislation down to the Act of Settlement of 1793.

In some towns it appears to have been practised with discrimination; that is, only such persons were warned to depart as the town authorities thought were likely to become in need of support. In other cases, however, it was apparently the practice to warn out all new-comers, whether thought likely to become chargeable or not.

The result of this was that a large number of persons became actual inhabitants of towns, owned property, paid taxes, held town offices, bore all the burdens and performed all the duties of citizenship, without ever acquiring the right of inhabitancy; that is, of support in case they or their children became in need of support. This fact and the uncertainty which arose in many such cases as to where the proper inhabitancy or settlement of persons who became in need of support was, led to the enactment of the General Law of Settlement of 1793.

The action of the Massachusetts towns in this matter is further illustrated by the following instances:—

In Marshfield in 1664 the town gave authority to the selectmen to warn idle or disorderly persons out of town, and the inhabitants were forbidden to entertain any person that had been so warned.†

---

*Compact, Charter and Laws of Colony of New Plymouth (edition 1836), p. 274.

† Richards, History of Marshfield, p. 48.

The records of Deerfield, May 11, 1664, show this notification:—

To the Selectmen of Deerfield: Gentlemen; This is to give Notice to you that there came to my House April 29th, 1664 Zebulen Tubbs his wife Esther Tubbs & two Children viz. Theuel & Esther where they now are. They came last from Hinsdale in the Province of New Hampshire their circumstances being something low in worldly things having no other estate that I know of but one Horse & two Cows.

JOHN HENRY.

A true Copy of ye Notification
  Attst Thos Williams T. Cler.

The forms of warning out used in Lancaster, Massachusetts, in 1671, show plainly that the warning out then practised was of such persons as were likely to become chargeable to the town.*

In this town, however, in 1791 the selectmen caused more than a hundred persons, men and women with their children, to be warned to depart out of the town without regard to their character or pecuniary condition. Among others thus treated was the Hon. John Sprague, who had been in town about twenty years, and had already represented the town in the General Court four years.

In 1679 the inhabitants of Salem were summoned to answer for permitting persons not inhabitants to abide in their houses. In 1679 two persons were authorized

to take an account of all inmates or strangers, that are now in or may hereafter come into the towne and returne their names to the selectmen every moneth, and, if need be, to warne them to depart.

In 1695 a "jersyman" (evidently a man from New Jersey) who had served six years in Salem was "warned"

---

* Nourse, *Annals of Lancaster*, p. 89.

Warning Out in New England 57

away. Such notices were frequent for twenty-five years after that time. Felt says that in 1790 and 1791 there were several hundred people in Salem not regular inhabitants who were warned to depart.*

In Reading in 1691 the record shows that three persons "were warned out of town." And this was done for many years thereafter, but confined, as it is said, to such new-comers as, in the opinion of the town, were likely to become a town charge.†

In Attleboro it was voted in 1697 that

> No person that is a stranger shall be received as an inhabitant without the consent or approbation of said Town, or sufficient security given to the Town by him or them that shall take in or harbor any person contrary to this order;—moreover the Selectmen are appointed to take due care and sufficient security in the behalf of the Town of and for all such persons as shall receive in or harbor any stranger or foriner, or to give order and warning to such stranger or foriner to depart the town according as the law directs, and that with all convenient speed after knowledge or notice given of the same.‡

In Medford it was the custom to warn every newcomer out of town, and record the notification in the Court of Sessions as a "caution" up to the time of the Revolution.§

The inhabitants of Sudbury repeatedly used the power of warning out strangers and of censuring and fining inhabitants who received strangers into their houses. They also ordered that no inhabitant should let or lease any houses or lands unto strangers without leave of the selectmen in a selectmen's meeting, or leave given in a general town meeting, unless they should "stake-down, depositate and bind over a suffi-

---

* Felt, *Annals of Salem*, Vol. I, pp. 358, 359, 360.
† Eaton, *History of Reading*, p. 36.
‡ Daggett, *History of Attleboro*, p. 88.
§ Usher, *History of Medford*, p. 111.

cient estate to the selectmen to save the town harmless from any charge that should come thereby."

They further provided that any violation of this order should be punished by a fine of nineteen shillings sixpence for each week's residence of the stranger, to be paid to the town.*

The records of Wenham show numerous instances of warning out, mostly soon after the Revolutionary War. One return upon a warrant reads: "I have warned said Margaret Poland, widow, to depart and leave the town, and Samuel Patch that he dont entertain her."†

In Canton the town warned out all new-comers, and made it the duty of all heads of families to inform the selectmen immediately of the name, age, occupation, and previous residence of the new-comer. One of these notifications in 1734 said of the new-comer,—

The Selectmen are informed that he has several hundred acres of land in Connecticut, but that a glass of good liquor stands a very narrow chance when it lies in his way.‡

In Dudley there is this record:—

To either of the Constables of the town of Dudley in the County of Worcester, *Greeting:*

Whereas, Martha MacKentiah of and belonging to Reading North precinct in the County of Essex has lately come into the sd town of Dudley with a child about two years old and the sd Martha being poor and in indigent circumstances may, if she be allowed to continue in sd town, become a charge to it—you are therefore hereby directed forthwith to warn the sd Martha MacKentiah, to depart with her child in the space of fourteen days, as she will answer the neglect at the peril of the law in that cause

---

* Hudson, *History of Sudbury,* pp. 138, 139.

† Allen, *History of Wenham,* p. 61.

‡ Huntoon, *History of Canton,* pp. 251, 252.

Warning Out in New England 59

made and provided given under our hands at Dudley the second day of August, Anno Domini, 1735.*

In Newbury the colony law with regard to the entertainment of strangers in towns was enforced by warning out and the imposition of penalties. Warrants were granted and served, warning new-comers out of town, and as late as 1734 the records of the selectmen show the payment to them of fines of forty shillings in each case for taking in "a tenant and not informing the Town's Clerk nor Selectmen of the Town of his so doing."†

In Lynn the practice prevailed for many years of warning out of the town by a warrant issued by the selectmen to every individual, rich or poor, who came into it. An amusing incident is related in the history of the town, arising under these orders. One elderly gentleman who had just arrived in town was served with an order to depart, and took it for a real intimation that they did not desire him to remain, and he said to his wife: "Come, wife, we must pack up. But there—we have one consolation for it, it is not so desirable a place."‡

In Tewksbury there was a case where a person, presumably a constable, appears to have warned himself out of town. The record shows this entry:—

To Daniel Pryor 18/, it being for warning himself and family and Mrs. Mahoney and her child, out of town.§

The returns of warnings out from the different towns in Worcester County from 1737 to 1788, on the records of the Court, show that 6,764 persons were thus warned

* *The Settlement of Dudley.* By Samuel Morris Conant. Quinabaug Historical Society leaflets, No. 8, p. 105.
 † Currier, *History of Newbury, Mass.*, pp. 216, 217.
 ‡ Lewis and Newhall, *History of Lynn*, p. 297.
 § Edward W. Pride, *In Tewksbury: A Short History*, p. 53.

out from forty different towns during that period. In some of the towns, it is said, a large proportion of the inhabitants appear in the list of persons warned, and many of them became prominent citizens in the towns.

The wording of the returns of the warrants, as recorded, is not uniform. The following are given as examples merely:—

Sturbridge Caution—against Saml Child, an old man now dwelling at the house of Moses Marcy Esq. Warrant dated Oct. 7.

The Selectmen of the Town of Sutton in said County are allowed to Enter their Caution against Kezia man the Selectmen refusing to admit her Inhabitant of said Town she having been duely warned thereout as by a Warrant under the Hands & Seal of the said Selectmen. Dated ye 23rd of December Last & Constables return thereon on file appears.*

In Haverhill it was customary to warn nearly all the new-comers to depart out of the town.†

In Lexington new-comers were warned out as early as 1714. The learned historian of the town, Charles Hudson, states the practice as follows:—

When any family or single person, even to a domestic in a family, came into town, the head of the family, or person owning the premises, was required to give notice to the selectmen of the names and numbers of the new comers, the place whence they came, the date of their coming into town, and their pecuniary condition. If the selectmen thought there was danger of their becoming a public charge, they caused them to be warned to leave the town, and to have a *caution*, as it was termed, entered with the Court of Sessions. This matter appears on our records as early as 1714, when "Capt. Joseph Estabrook was authorized to request the Honorable Court of Sessions in June next, to enter cautions against Daniel Cutting and his wife, Sarah Cook, and Johanna Snow, that they might not be burthensome to Lex-

---

* Blake, *Worcester County Warnings*, 1899.
† *History of Haverhill*, p. 229.

ington." In 1722, Daniel Roff with his family were ordered to depart out of Lexington. We will add a few specimens of these notices:—

LEXINGTON, Jan. 6, 1761.

To the Selectmen. Gentlemen: These are to inform you that on the 19th of December last past, I took widow Elizabeth Sampson, as a housekeeper, from Harvard, that being her last place of residence; she being under good circumstances.

JOHN BRIDGE.

To the Selectment of the Town of Lexington.

Gent: These are to inform you that I have received into my house to reside with me, Abigail Stone, on or about ye 12th of May. Her last place of residence, Woburn. Her circumstances I believe are low. JAMES ROBBINS.

May 29, 1762.

At December Court, 1760, Caution was entered against Edmand Dix, Hannah Stockbridge, Ann Hodge, and Hannah Ross, as the law directs.

Widow Abigail Whittemore informs—that on the 26th day of December, 1755, she took into her house as inmates her son-in-law, Nathaniel Whittemore, with his wife and child, under poor circumstances. They came from Lincoln. She informed, Jan. 5, 1756.

At a meeting of the Selectmen, Aug. 27, 1744, Allowed Constable Daniel Brown, 3 shillings for warning Richard Hutchinson out of town.

Also ordered the Clerk to draw a warrant and give it to the Constable to warn Archable Mackintosh and his family, forthwith to depart out of Lexington.

These examples, which are taken promiscuously from the records, show the manner in which business was done at that time, and the general supervision which the authorities took of public, or as some might say, private affairs. It seems by the examples that a gentleman could not hire a man to live with him, or a girl to work in his family, or allow a tenant to occupy his house, or a house under his care, without giving notice thereof to the selectmen. And it is worthy of remark that these notices have been given of the incoming of certain individuals, who have afterwards become some of the most respectable and influential men in the town. Some of the young women whose ingress into town was thus publicly heralded, won the hearts of some of the permanent residents, and became the mothers of some of Lexington's most honored citizens. And when the calls of our country required the services of her patriotic sons, several of the very men who had been "warned out of town," were among the first to obey the call.*

In Bridgewater it was the custom much in use to warn out all persons moving into town. The notice was served by a constable, usually in the following form:—

By virtue of a warrant from the Selectmen of the town of Bridgewater you are requested to depart the limits of said town within fifteen days, you never having obtained leave of inhabiting the same.†

November 25, 1789.

In Oxford, beginning in 1789, when the town had become poor and the number of indigent persons had increased in consequence of the Revolution, the custom of warning out was adopted with reference to all newcomers. In December, 1789, a man and his family and "a spinster" from other towns were warned to leave town, "they having come for the purpose of abiding therein not having obtained the town's consent therefor."

In February, 1792, 78 persons were warned out of town; in the following June, 23; and December, 1793, 42.‡

In Greenfield, beginning about 1790, warning out was quite generally practised, and the town records show that the ancestors of very well-known families at present time were warned to depart, but remained.

The same practice was followed in Bernardston, where in 1790 eight men "coming from Greenfield" were warned to depart out of town.

* Hudson, *History of Lexington*, p. 80.
† Kingman, *History of North Bridgewater*, p. 346.
‡ Daniels, *History of Oxford*, p. 769.

CHAPTER IV.

INHABITANCY AND WARNING OUT IN CONNECTICUT.—EARLY COLONY AND STATE LAWS.—ILLUSTRATIONS OF ACTION OF TOWNS, ETC.

In no part of New England was the admission of inhabitants, transfer of land, and warning out of persons who sought to be inhabitants without being admitted by the towns more carefully guarded than in Connecticut. The early laws passed by the General Court for the Colony were very strict and specific with regard to these matters. By subsequent additions to and amendments of these early statutes the Connecticut Code of Laws with regard to admission of inhabitants, liability of support for those admitted, and with regard to removing persons who came into towns without being admitted, was more elaborate, complicated, and severe, than that of any other New England Colony or State. For this reason and because these early laws are not easily accessible I have thought it best to reproduce these statutes at length, although some of the provisions contained in them may not be of particular importance as bearing upon the matter of warning out.*

The admission of inhabitants was carefully provided for by the "Fundamentals," so called, adopted at Hartford, January 14, 1638. The first one of these provided that the choice of officers

---

* The early laws of Connecticut were compiled and printed in 1702, but only two complete copies are now known to exist. From one of these copies the Acorn Society of Hartford published a reprint in 1901, in an edition of one hundred copies. It is from this reprint that the citations are here made.

shall be made by all that are admitted freemen and haue taken the Oath of Fidelity, and doe cohabitte w^{th}in this Jurisdiction, (hauing beene admitted Inhabitants by the maior p^rt of the Towne wherein they liue,) or the mayor p^rte of such as shall be then p^rsent.

The words in parentheses are not in the original record, but were interlined in a different handwriting at a later period. Presumably this was done after 1643, for we find this record on November 10, 1643:—

> Whereas in the fundamentall Order yt is said (that such who haue taken the Oath of fidellity and are admitted inhabitants) shall be alowed as quallified for chuseing of Deputyes, The Court declares their judgement, that such only shall be counted admitted inhabitants, who are admitted by a generall voate of the mayor p^rte of the Towne that receaueth them.*

Again at a joint Court † on February 26, 1656, the qualifications of inhabitants were stated by the following order:—

> This Court doth order, that by admitted inhabitants, specified in the 7th Fundamentall, are meant only housholders that are one & twenty yeares of age, or haue bore office, or haue 30*l.* estate.

The 7th Fundamental here referred to was the one providing for the choice of deputies by all that were admitted inhabitants in the several towns.‡

May 17, 1660, it was ordered by the General Court that

> None shalbe receaued as Inhabitant into any Towne in the Collony but such as are knowne to be of an honest conversation, and accepted by a maior part of the Towne.
>
> It is alsoe ordered, that noe Inhabitant shall haue power to

---

* *Public Records of the Colony of Connecticut*, Vol. I, pp. 21, 96.

† "The magistrates and deputies then met together and acted jointly as one body. They first acted as two bodies in October, 1698." Trumbull, p. 399.

‡ *Ibid.*, p. 293.

make sale of his assomodat^n of house and lands vntil he haue first propounded the sale thereof to ye Towne where it is situate and they refuse to accept of ye sale tendred.*

In the laws of 1673 it was provided that every town should maintain their own poor, and also that

If any person come to live in any Town in this Government, and be there received and entertained three months, if by sickness, lameness or the like, he comes to want reliefe; he shall be provided for by that Town wherin he was so long entertained, and shall be reputed their proper charge, unless such person have within the said three months been warned by the Constable, or some one or more of the Select men of that Town, not there to abide without leave first obtained of the Town, and certifie the same to the next Court of Assistants, who shall othersise Order the charge arising about him according to Justice.†

By the laws of 1702 it was

ORDERED AND ENACTED That no inhabitant in this Colony, shall have power to make sale of his Accomodations, of House or Lands, to any but the Inhabitants of the Township wherein the said House and Lands is Scituate, without the consent of the Town, and unless he have first propounded the Sale thereof, to the Town, where it is Scituate and they refuse the Sale tendred, or to give so much as another Chapman will.‡

It was also provided that

WHEREAS several persons of an Ungoverned Conversation, thrust themselves into our Townships, and by some under hand way, as either upon pretence of being hired Servants, or of hiring Lands or Houses, become inhabitants in our Townships, whereby much Inconveniency doth arise to such places, such persons often proving vicious, chargeable and burthensome to the places where they come: which to prevent,

IT IS ENACTED AND ORDAINED That no person shall be received an Inhabitant into any Town in this Colony, but such as are

---

* Trumbull, p. 351.
† *The Laws of Connecticut*, 1673, p. 57.
‡ *Acts and Laws of Colony of Connecticut*, 1702, p. 53.

known to be of an honest Conversation, and accepted by the major part of the Town.

And that no transient person shall be allowed to Reside, and make his or her abode in any Township in this Colony, (Apprentices under age, and Servants bought for time excepted) upon pretence of Hiring, or being Hired, or Tennantship or Inmates, without the approbation of the Authority, and Select-men of such Town.

And if any person or persons shall contrary to the intent of this Act, entertain or hire any stranger or transient person, or Lett any House or Land to such stranger or transient person, except he or they shall first give good security to the acceptance of the said Authority, and Select-men, that such Town or Plantation shall not be burthened and charged by him or them, he shall forfeit and pay to the use of the poor of the Town whereto he or they belong, the Sum of Twenty Shillings per Week, for every Week, he shall harbour, entertain, or hire any such person.

AND IT IS FURTHER ENACTED AND ORDAINED That the Civil Authority, when and so often as there shall be occasion in any Town or Plantation in this Colony, shall be, and are hereby Impowered to order any vagrant or suspected person or persons, to be sent back from Constable to Constable, to the place or places from whence he or they came; unless such person or persons can produce good Certificate, that he or they are persons of good behaviour, free from all ingagements, and at liberty to remove themselves as he or they shall see meet: and if such person shall return after they are sent back as aforesaid, and abide and continue in said Town after warning given them to depart, they shall be severely Whipt, not exceeding Ten Stripes.*

And it was further

ENACTED, That if any person or persons shall come to live in any Town in this Colony, and be there received and entertained by the space of three months, and if by Sickness, lameness, or the like, he or they come to want relief, every such person or persons shall be provided for by that Town wherein he or they was so long entertained, at their own proper charge; unless such person or persons have within the said three months, been warned by the Constable, or some one or more of the Select-men of that Town,

---

* *Acts and Laws of Colony of Connecticut,* 1702, p. 58.

to depart and leave the place: which if the said Constable, or any one or more of the Select-men shall do, and thereof certifie the next Court of Assistants to be held in this Colony, the said Court of Assistants shall and may otherwise order the defraying of the Charge arising about such person or persons.*

In 1750 it was provided that

If any Person, or Persons shall come to Live in any Town in this Colony, and be there Received, and Entertained by the space of Three Months: and if by Sickness, Lameness, or the like, he, or they come to want Relief, every such Person, or Persons shall be Provided for by that Town wherein he, or they were so long Entertained, at said Towns own proper Cost, and Charge; Unless such Person, or Persons by Law are to be provided for by any particular Inhabitant of such Town: Or unless such Person, or Persons wanting Relief have within the said Three Months been Warned as the Law directs, to Depart, and Leave the Place: And if such Warning be given, and the same be Certified to the next Superiour Court to be held in the same County, the said Court shall, and may otherwise Order the Defraying the Charge arising about such Indigent Person, or Persons.†

In 1769 an Act for the admission of inhabitants in towns, and for the preventing of charge on account of such as are not admitted therein, was passed as follows:—

WHEREAS several Persons of ungoverned Conversation, thrust themselves into the Towns in this Colony, and by some underhand Way, as upon pretence of being hired Servants; or of hiring Lands or Houses; or by purchasing the same, endeavour to become Inhabitants in such Towns.

And whereas Persons are sometimes Entertained, and set to Work by those who live in the Skirts and obscure Places of said Towns, out of the View and Observation of the Officers of the Town, whereby much Inconvenience doth arise; such Persons often proving Vicious, and Chargeable and Burthensome to the Places where they come.

* *Acts and Laws of Colony of Connecticut,* 1702, p. 95.
† *Acts and Laws of Connecticut in New-England in America,* 1750, p. 191.

Which to prevent:

Be it Enacted by the Governour, Council and Representatives, in General Court assembled, and by the Authority of the same, That no Person shall be received or admitted an Inhabitant in any Town in this Colony, but such as are known to be of an honest Conversation, and shall be accepted by the major Part of the Town; or by the Authority in, and Select-men of the Town.

That no Stranger or transient Person shall be allowed to reside, and make his or her Abode in any Town in this Colony, (Apprentices under Age, and Servants bought for Time excepted) upon pretence of hiring, of being hired, or of Tenantship, or Inmates, without the approbation of the Authority in, and the Select-men of such Town.

And the more effectually to prevent Persons from making their Abode in any Town contrary to this Act.

Be it further Enacted by the Authority aforesaid, That if any Person or Persons shall contrary to the intent of this Act, entertain or hire any Stranger or transient Person; or Let any House or Land to such Stranger or transient Person; except he or they shall first give Security to the acceptance of the said Authority and Select-men, that such Town shall not be Burthened and Charged by him or them, (which Security such Authority and Selectmen may take or refuse at their Discretion) he or they so entertaining or hiring or Letting any House or Land to such Stranger, or transient Person, shall forfeit and pay to the Treasurer of the Town whereto he or they belong, the Sum of *Ten Shillings* per Week, for every Week he or they shall Harbour, Entertain, Hire, or Let such Estate to such Person.

And if any such Stranger, or transient Person, shall contrary to the intent of this Act, make his or her Abode within any Town in this Colony, every such Person shall forfeit and pay to such Treasurer *Ten Shillings* per Week for every Week that he or she shall continue in such Town after warning given to him or her, by Order of the Select-men of said Town; or upon their Request, by Warrant from Authority to Depart such Town, (which Warning the said Select-men are Impowred to order, or give: And the said Authority, on Request, as aforesaid, is Impowred to issue a Warrant to the Constable, to warn such Persons to Depart as aforesaid.)

And when it shall so happen that any such Stranger, or transient Person, who shall be Convicted of the Breach of this Act,

Warning Out in New England 69

and hath not Estate to satisfy the Fine, such Person shall be Whipped upon the naked Body, not exceeding Ten Stripes; unless he or she Depart the Town within Ten Days next after Sentence given, and reside no more therein without Leave of the Selectmen.

Any one Assistant, or Justice of the Peace to hear and determine the Breach of this Act.

Provided nevertheless, That if such Stranger, or transient Person hath continued in any Town for the space of One Year before such Warning given, or shall continue in such Town One Year after such Warning, and be not in that Time prosecuted for Breach of this Act, then it shall not be Lawful to proceed against, or prosecute any such Person by Virtue of this Act, for continuing in such Town contrary to the same; but such Person may continue in such Town this Act notwithstanding.

Be it further Enacted by the Authority aforesaid, That whosoever shall entertain any such Stranger, or transient Person or Persons for the space of Four Days, and the said Person shall while so Entertained be reduced by Sickness, or other Accident to necessitous Circumstances, whereby he, she, or they shall want Relief, the Person so entertaining such Stranger, or transient Person or Persons shall Support and Sustain the Charge thereof; excepting only when the Person Entertaining, as aforesaid, hath within the said Four Days, given sufficient Notice thereof to the Select-men of the Town: In which Case, if the Select-men do not use proper Methods to save the Town from Charge, then it shall be defrayed by such Town.

Be it further Enacted by the Authority aforesaid, That if any Person or Persons within any Town in this Colony, shall sell, or convey any Land to any Person or Persons, who contrary to this Act would under Colour of such Purchase make his, her or their Abode in such Town; he or they Selling, as aforesaid, shall for every such Offence forfeit, and pay as a Fine, the Sum of *Ten Pounds:* One Moiety to the Town Treasurer where such Land lies; and the other Half to him who shall Complain of, and Prosecute the same to Effect.

And be it further Enacted by the Authority aforesaid, That the Civil Authority, when and so often as there shall be Occasion in any Town, shall be, and they are hereby Impowred, to Order any Vagrant, or Suspected, or transient Person or Persons to be sent back from Constable to Constable, to the Town, Place, or Places from whence he, she, or they came; unless such Person or Persons produce good Certificate of their good Behaviour and Freedom from all Engagements, and that they are at liberty to remove themselves as they see meet.

And if any such Persons shall return after such sending back, as aforesaid, and abide and continue in said Town from whence sent, after Warning given them to Depart, they shall be Whipt on the naked Body, not exceeding Ten Stripes: And may again be sent, and dealt with as aforesaid, as often as there shall be Occasion.

And the Select-men in the respective Towns in this Colony, are hereby Impowred and Directed to prosecute all Breaches of this Act.*

In 1784 an Act was passed for the admission of inhabitants in towns and for preventing charge on account of such as are not admitted therein, as follows:—

Be it enacted by the Governor, Council and Representatives, in General Court assembled, and by the Authority of the same, That no transient Person or Inhabitant of any other State, who may come to reside or dwell in any Town in this State, shall gain a legal Settlement in such Town by dwelling there, unless admitted by a major Vote of the Inhabitants of such Town, or by Consent of the civil Authority in and Select-men of said Town, or unless such Persons shall be appointed and execute some Public Office, or have been possessed in his own Right in Fee of a real Estate of the Value of One Hundred Pounds in such Town, during his Continuance there; but such Persons, not having gained a Settlement as aforesaid, if the Select-men judge they are likely to become chargeable to said Town, may be removed to the Place of their last legal Settlement, notwithstanding any length of Time that they may have been suffered to continue in such Town.

That no Person shall be received or admitted an Inhabitant in any Town in this State, but such as are known to be of an honest Conversation, and shall be accepted by the major Part of the Town, or by the Authority in and Select-men of the Town. And no Stranger or transient Person shall be allowed to reside

---

* *Acts and Laws of His Majesty's English Colony of Connecticut in New-England in America*, 1769, pp. 99, 100, 101.

or make his or her Abode in any Town in this State, (Apprentices under age and Servants bought for Time excepted) upon Pretence of hiring or being hired, or of Tenantship, or Inmates without the Approbation of the Authority in and Select-men of such Town.

That if any Person or Persons shall contrary to the Intent of this Act, entertain or hire any Stranger or transient Person, or let any House or Land to such Stranger or transient Person, except he or they shall first give Security to the Acceptance of the said Authority and Select-men, that such Town shall not be burthened and charged by him or them; which Security such Authority and Select-men may take or refuse at their Discretion; he or they so entertaining, or hiring, or letting any House or Land to such Stranger or transient Person, shall forfeit and pay to the Treasurer of such Town, the Sum of *Ten Shillings per Week*, for every Week he or they shall harbour, entertain, hire, or let such Estate to such Person.

And if any such Stranger or transient Person shall, contrary to the Intent of this Act, make his or her Abode within any Town in this State, every such Person shall forfeit and pay to such Treasurer *Ten Shillings* per Week, for every Week that he or she shall continue in such Town, after Warning given to him or her, by order of the Select-men of said Town; or upon their Request, by Warrant from Authority to depart such Town, (which Warning the Select-men are impowered to order, or give:) And the said Authority, on Request as aforesaid, is impowered to issue a Warrant to the Constable, to warn such Persons to depart, as aforesaid.

And when any such Stranger or transient Person, who shall be convicted of the Breach of this Act, and hath no Estate to satisfy the Fine, such Person shall be whipped upon his naked Body, not exceeding Ten Stripes; unless he or she depart the Town within Ten Days next after Sentence given, and reside no more therein without Leave of the Select-men.

Any one Assistant or Justice of the Peace, to hear and determine the Breach of this Act.

Be it further enacted by the Authority aforesaid, That whosoever shall entertain such Stranger or transient Person or Persons, for the Space of Four Days, and the said Person shall, when so entertained, be reduced by Sickness, or other Accident, to necessitous Circumstances, whereby he, she or they shall want

Relief, the Person so entertaining such Stranger or transient Person or Persons, shall support and sustain the Charge thereof; excepting only when the Person entertaining as aforesaid, hath within the said Four Days, given sufficient Notice thereof to the Select-men of the Town; in which Case, if the Select-men do not use proper Methods to save the Town from Charge, then it shall be defrayed by such Town.

Be it further enacted by the Authority aforesaid, That if any Person or Persons within any Town in this State, shall sell or convey any Land to any Person or Persons, who contrary to this Act, would under Colour of such Purchase, make his, her or their Abode in such Town; he or they selling as aforesaid, shall for every such Offence, forfeit and pay as a Fine, the Sum of *Ten Pounds:* one Moiety to the Town Treasury where such Land lies, and the other Half to him who shall complain of and prosecute the same to Effect.

And be it further enacted by the Authority aforesaid, That the civil Authority, when and so often as there shall be Occasion in any Town, shall be, and they are hereby impowered to order any Vagrant, suspected or transient Person or Persons to be sent back, from Constable to Constable, to the Town, Place or Places from whence he, she or they came; unless such Person or Persons produce good Certificates of their good Behaviour, and Freedom from all Engagements, and that they are at Liberty to remove themselves as they shall see meet. . . .

And that said Authority may in like Manner remove any Stranger or transient Person or Persons who shall neglect or refuse, or be unable to depart such Town after Warning given, as before in this Act is provided.

And if any such Persons shall return after such sending back, as aforesaid, and abide and continue in said Town from whence sent, after Warning given them to depart, they shall be whipt on the naked Body, not exceeding ten Stripes; and may again be sent and dealt with as aforesaid, as often as there shall be Occasion.

And the Select-men in the respective Towns in this State, are hereby impowered and directed to prosecute all Breaches of this Act.

And be it further enacted, That any Inhabitant of any Town within this State, may, for the better Support of himself or Family, have Liberty to remove with his Family into any other

Town in this State, and continue there without being liable to be removed, provided such Person procure a Certificate in Writing, under the Hands of the civil Authority in and Select-men of the Town from whence he removes, that he is a legal Inhabitant in that Town, and lodge the same with the Clerk of the Town to which he removes. And in Case such Person or any of his Family, stand in Need of Relief from said Town, he or they shall be supported at the Cost of the Town where such Person was setteled and obtained a Certificate as aforesaid; and may be returned back to such Town, provided such Person hath not been admitted an Inhabitant, or gained a Settlement, as before in this Act is provided, in any other Town, after such Certificate was given.

Provided nevertheless, That Persons coming to reside in any Town as aforesaid, they and their Estates shall be as liable to be taken under the Care of the Select-men of the Town where they dwell, for Mismanagement, Idleness or bad Husbandry, agreeable to the Law in that Case provided, as if they had a legal Settlement in such Town; and nothing in this Act shall be construed to hinder such Towns from ridding themselves of any Vagrant, or Persons whom such Town, or the Authority therein, or the Select-men thereof shall judge to be of disorderly, ungoverned or vicious Conversation.

And be it further enacted, That any Inhabitant of any Town in this State, who shall go to reside in any other Town in this State, without having a Certificate as aforesaid, may be removed and sent back to the Town to which he or she belongs, in like Manner as is before provided in this Act for the Removal of any Stranger, or transient Person: Provided such Person shall not have continued in such Town one Year before Warning given to depart, or one Year after such Warning, without being prosecuted as aforesaid.*

In 1792 an Act in addition to and alteration of an Act entitled "An Act for the admission of Inhabitants in Towns, and for preventing charge on account of such as are admitted therein," was passed as follows:—

Be it enacted by the Governor, Council, and Representatives in General Court assembled, and by the authority of the same,

* *Acts and Laws of Connecticut,* 1784, pp. 102-104.

That the provisions of said Act notwithstanding, any Inhabitant of any Town in this State may remove with his or her family; or if such person has no family, may remove him or herself into any other Town in this State, and continue there, without being liable to be warned to depart, or to be removed therefrom, except in the case herein after provied; and shall gain a legal settlement in the Town to which he or she may have so removed, in case he or she shall reside in such Town for the full term of six years next, from and after his or her first removal into such Town; and shall during the whole of said term, have supported him or herself, and his or her family; if such person have a family at the time of said first removal, or at any time during said term, without his, her, or their becoming chargeable to such Town, or to the Town that may by law be liable to charge for the support of such person and family; but if any such person shall at any time before the expiration of said term of six years, become unable to support and maintain him or herself, and family, if any be, and chargeable to the Town, that may be liable to charge for his, her or their support; in that case every such person with his or her family, if any be, may be removed to the place of his or her last legal settlement, in manner as in said Act is already provided.

And be it further enacted, That any person who shall bring into this State, any poor and indigent person, and leave him or her in any Town within the same, of which Town he or she is not an inhabitant, such person so bringing in and leaving such poor and indigent person, shall forfeit and pay, for every such person so brought in, and left, the sum of Twenty Pounds lawful money, to be recovered in any Court proper to try the same, to, and for the use of such Towne.*

In 1796 a Settlement Act was passed, providing how inhabitants might be admitted into towns, as follows:—

AN ACT FOR THE ADMISSION OF INHABITANTS IN TOWNS AND FOR PREVENTING CHARGE ON ACCOUNT OF SUCH AS ARE NOT ADMITTED THEREIN.

Par. 1. Be it enacted by the Governor and Council, and House of Representatives, in General Court assembled, That no Person

* *Connecticut Laws*, 1784 to 1792, p. 412.

who is not an Inhabitant of this State, or of any of the United States, who may come to reside in any Town in this State, shall gain a legal Settlement in such Town, unless admitted by Vote of the Inhabitants of such Town, or by Consent of the Civil Authority in, and Select-men of such Town, or unless such Person shall be appointed to and execute some public Office.

2. Be it further enacted, That no Person who is an Inhabitant of any of the United States (this State excepted) who may come to reside in any Town in this State, shall gain a legal Settlement therein, unless he have some one of the Requisites enumerated in the preceding Paragraph, or unless he shall have been possessed in his own Right in fee of a real Estate of the value of Three Hundred and Thirty-four Dollars, during his continuance there, but such Person not having gained a Settlement as aforesaid, if the Select-men judge he is likely to become chargeable to such Town, may be removed to the Place of his last legal Settlement, as is hereafter in this Act provided.

3. Be it further enacted, That no Inhabitant of any Town in this State, shall gain a legal Settlement in any other Town in this State, unless he have some one of the Requisites enumerated in the first Paragraph of this Act, or unless he shall have been possessed in his own Right, in Fee of a real Estate of the Value of One Hundred Dollars, in the Town to which he may have removed, during his Continuance therein, or unless he hath supported himself for the Term of six Years, agreeably to a subsequent Provision in this Act.

4. Be it further enacted, That any Inhabitant of any Town in this State, may remove with his or her Family, or if such Person have no Family, may remove him or herself into any other Town in this State, and continue there without being liable to be warned to depart, or to be removed therefrom, except in the Case herein after provided; and shall gain a legal Settlement in the Town to which he or she may have so removed, in Case he or she shall reside in such Town, for the full Term of six Years next, from and after his or her first removal into such Town; and shall during the whole of said Term, have supported him or herself, and his or her Family; if such Person have a Family at the time of said first removal, or at any Time during said Term, without his, her, or their becoming Chargeable to such Town, or to the Town that may by law be liable to Charge for the Support of such Person and Family; but if any such Person shall at any Time before the

Expiration of said Term of six Years, become unable to support and maintain him or herself and Family, if any be, and become chargeable to the Town, that may be liable to charge for his, her, or their Support; in that Case every such Person, with his or her Family, if any be, may be removed to the Place of his or her last legal Settlement, in the same Manner as is hereafter provided in this Act, respecting the removal of Inhabitants of other States.*

5. Be it further enacted, That when an Inhabitant of any of the United States (this State excepted) shall come to reside in any Town in this State, the Civil Authority or major part of them in such Town are hereby authorized (upon the application of the Select-men) if they judge proper, by warrant under their hands directed to either of the Constables of said Town, to order said Person to be conveyed to the State, from whence he or she came; and such Constable on receiving said Warrant, is hereby authorized to execute the same, and the Expence thereof being liquidated and allowed by the Select-men of the Town to which such Constable belongs, shall be paid out of the Treasury of such Town. And also the Expence of conveying an Inhabitant of this State as aforesaid, shall be liquidated, allowed and paid in the same Manner; Provided such Person in either Case has not gained a legal Settlement as aforesaid.

6. Be it further enacted, That the Select-men of any Town be, and they are hereby authorized, either by themselves, or by Warrant from an Assistant or Justice of the Peace, in such Town, directed to either Constable of such Town, which Warrant such Assistant or Justice is hereby authorized to give, to warn any Person not an Inhabitant of this State, to depart such Town, and the Person so warned, shall forfeit and pay to the Treasurer of such Town, One Dollar and Sixty-seven Cents per Week, for every Week he or she shall continue in such Town, after Warning given as aforesaid; and when any such Person who shall be convicted of the Breach of this Act, in refusing to depart on Warning as aforesaid, hath no Estate to satisfy the Fine, such Person shall be whipped on the naked Body not exceeding ten Stripes, unless he or she depart the Town within ten Days next after Sentence given, and reside no more therein, without leave of the Select-men. Provided nevertheless, That nothing contained in this Paragraph, or the Paragraph next preceeding, shall be con-

* The foregoing paragraph was enacted in May, 1792.

strued to effect Apprentices under Age, or Servants bought for Time.

7. Be it further enacted, That if any Person not an Inhabitant of this State, shall return after such sending away as aforesaid, and abide in said Town from whence sent, after Warning given him to depart as aforesaid, he shall be whipped on the naked Body not exceeding ten Stripes, and may again be sent away, and dealt with as aforesaid, as often as there shall be Occasion; and the Select-men in the respective Towns are hereby empowered and directed to prosecute all Breaches of this Act.

8. Be it further enacted, That if any Inhabitant in any Town, shall contrary to the intent of this Act, entertain or hire any such Person not an Inhabitant of this State, who shall come to reside in such Town, or let any House or Land to such Person, unless such Inhabitant shall first give Security to the Acceptance of the Authority and Select-men of such Town, to save said Town from all Expence that might be occasioned thereby; such Inhabitant shall forfeit and pay to the Treasury of such Town, One Dollar and Sixty-seven Cents, per Week, for every Week he or she shall harbor, entertain, hire, or let Estate as aforesaid.

9. Be it further enacted, That any Person who shall bring into this State any poor and indigent Person, and leave him or her in any Town within the same, of which Town he or she is not an Inhabitant, such Person so bringing in and leaving such poor and indigent Person, shall forfeit and pay for every such Person so brought in and left, the Sum of Sixty-seven Dollars, to be recovered in any Court proper to try the same, to and for the Use of such Town.

10. Be it further enacted, That whosoever shall entertain any Person not an Inhabitant of any Town in this State, for the space of fourteen Days, and the said Person shall, when so entertained, be reduced by Sickness, or otherwise, to necessitous Circumstances, so as to need Relief, the Person so entertaining shall support and sustain the Charge thereof, excepting only when he hath within the said fourteen Days, given sufficient Notice thereof to the Select-men of the Town in which such Person is so entertained, in which Case it shall be defrayed out of the public Treasury of this State, by Order of the Governor and Council, (unless the Person so entertained hath Relations who by Law are liable for his Support) and all Expence that may be incurred in the Support of such Person within the Term of three Months, from

the Time of his coming to such Town, in Case he shall within the Term of three Months, have been warned to depart said Town, shall in like Manner be defrayed out of the public Treasury of this State, and all Expences that may arise in Support of such Person, subsequent to the said Term of three Months, on account of Sickness or Lameness, which shall have commenced within the said Term of three Months, and which shall have continued beyond the said Term, to such a Degree as to render it unsafe to remove such Person, shall during the continuance of such Sickness or Lameness only, be defrayed out of the public Treasury of this State, and all subsequent Expences shall be defrayed by such Town, during his continuance therein.

11. Be it further enacted, That the several Towns in this State, shall be holden to support and maintain their respective Inhabitants, whether living within the Towns to which they belong, or in any other Town in this State, who may need Relief, and any Town which shall have pursuant to the Provisions of this Act, incurred Expence in supporting the Inhabitants of any other Town, shall have Liberty in Addition to the Provision already made, to bring any proper Action at common Law against the said Town for the recovery of such Expence.*

It will be seen that this Act prevented any person not an inhabitant of Connecticut, or of any of the United States (*i.e.*, a foreigner), from becoming a legal inhabitant of a town except by vote of the inhabitants of the town or consent of the civil authority and selectmen without such vote, or by being appointed to and executing some public office. It also prevented any inhabitant of the United States except Connecticut from becoming a legal inhabitant of a town without being admitted in the manner provided for foreigners, or being possessed of real estate in fee to the value of $334.

It also provided that no inhabitant of Connecticut should become a legal inhabitant in any town unless he was admitted by the town or the author-

* *Acts and Laws of the State of Connecticut*, 1796, p. 239.

ities, or appointed to and executed a public office, or possessed of real estate in fee of the value of $100, or should have resided in and supported himself and family in the town for the full term of six years next from and after first coming into the town. This practically repealed the law as to warning persons living in Connecticut to depart from any town into which they might remove.

As to inhabitants of the United States coming into any town in Connecticut, the Act provided that the civil authority of the town, being the justices of the peace, might upon application of the selectmen cause them to be conveyed out of Connecticut to the State from whence they came. The Act also provided that the selectmen might by warrant to a constable of the town "warn any person not an inhabitant of this state to depart such town," and that the "person so warned should forfeit to the Treasurer of the town $1.67 a week for every week he remained in town after the warning." The Act also provided that any person who should be convicted of refusing to depart when warned, who had no estate to satisfy the fine, should be "whipped on the naked body not exceeding ten stripes, unless he or she depart the town within ten days next after sentence, and reside no more therein without leave of the selectmen." And the Act further provided that any person warned out, who went away and then returned, should be "whipped on the naked body not exceeding ten stripes and again sent away," and "dealt with as aforesaid as often as there shall be occasion."

This Act further provided that no inhabitant in any town should entertain or hire any person not an inhabitant of Connecticut who should come to reside in such town, or let any house or land to such person without security first given to the acceptance of the civil authority and selectmen of the town to save the town from all expense that might be occasioned thereby, under a penalty of $1.67 a week for every week that any inhabitant "should harbour, entertain, hire or let estate" to such new-comer, and also provided that whoever should entertain any person not being an inhabitant of any town in the State for fourteen days, should be chargeable with the support of such person unless within the fourteen days he gave notice thereof to the selectmen of the town, and that if within three months of the time of his coming into town such newcomer should be warned to depart the town, then the charges of his support should be paid by the State during said three months, and during such further time as it might be unsafe on account of sickness or lameness of the person to remove him from the town, and that otherwise all subsequent expense beyond said three months from the time of warning should be paid by the town.*

Such were the provisions of the law of a Christian State, and they were substantially re-enacted in 1805.†

The provision as to removal of any inhabitant of any other State than Connecticut from a town in the State, and the provision for warning out any person not an inhabitant of the State, and also the provision against entertaining or hiring or letting any house or land to any person not an inhabitant of the State, were retained in the successive revisions of the statutes in 1821, 1835, 1849, 1854, 1866, 1875, and 1888, except that in 1835 the provision that any person warned out who should refuse to depart and have no estate to satisfy the fine of $1.67 a week, whenever he

* *Acts and Laws of Connecticut*, 1796, p. 239.
† *Connecticut Laws*, 1805, pp. 239, 294.

Warning Out in New England 81

or she continued in town after the warning, should be whipped on the naked body, not exceeding ten stripes, etc., was repealed. The repeal was found, however, in an Act to prevent the setting up of schools for the instruction of colored persons from other States, which provided that

WHEREAS, attempts have been made to establish literary institutions in this state for the instruction of colored persons belonging to other states and countries, which would tend to the great increase of the colored population of the state, and thereby to the injury of the people: Therefore,

BE *it enacted by the Senate and House of Representatives in General Assembly convened.* SECT. 1. That no person shall set up or establish in this state any school, academy, or literary institution, for the instruction or education of colored persons who are not inhabitants of this state, nor instruct or teach in any school, academy, or other literary institution whatsoever in this state, or harbor or board, for the purpose of attending or being taught or instructed in any such school, academy, or literary institution, any colored person who is not an inhabitant of any town in this state without, the consent, in writing, first obtained of a majority of the civil authority, and also of the select-men of the town in which such school, academy, or literary institution is situated; and each and every person who shall knowingly do any act forbidden as aforesaid, or shall be aiding or assisting therein, shall, for the first offence, forfeit and pay to the treasurer of this state, a fine of one hundred dollars, and for the second offence shall forfeit and pay a fine of two hundred dollars, and so double for every offence of which he or she shall be convicted. And all informing officers are required to make due presentment of all breaches of this act.*

And also except that in 1854 the provision that any person not an inhabitant of Connecticut, who should return after having been warned out, should be whipped on the naked body and again sent away, and whipped again so often as he might come back, was omitted from the statute; and that in 1888 the provision that

* *Public Statute Laws of Connecticut,* 1835, Title 53, p. 321.

any inhabitant of any other State than Connecticut might be conveyed out of the State was modified so that such person could be removed only if he became chargeable for support in the town within the first year of his residence therein.*

The Connecticut Settlement Act now in force provides for the admission of inhabitants by vote of the towns or consent of its justices of the peace and selectmen, and prevents any person not an inhabitant of Connecticut or of the United States from obtaining a settlement in any other way.

It also preserves the distinction between the inhabitants of other States and inhabitants of Connecticut by providing a different property qualification and a different term of residence to acquire a settlement. Inhabitants of other States must have resided in the town one year, and have been admitted by vote of the town, or have resided in the town one year and have been possessed in fee of unencumbered real estate in Connecticut to the value of $334. Inhabitants of Connecticut can gain a legal settlement in a town in that State only by being admitted by vote of the inhabitants or by having resided four years continuously in the town without becoming chargeable for support of the town.

In short, inhabitants of other States can obtain settlements either by being admitted by vote of the town or by residing in the town one year and being possessed of unencumbered real estate to the value of $334. Inhabitants of other towns in Connecticut can gain settlement either by being admitted by vote of

---

* *Public Statute Laws of Connecticut*, 1821, p. 236 et seq.; *Public Statute Laws of Connecticut*, 1835, p. 317 et seq.; *Revised Statutes of Connecticut*, 1849, p. 535; *The Statutes of Connecticut*, 1854, p. 717; *General Statutes of Connecticut*, 1866, p. 619; *General Statutes of Connecticut*, Revision 1875, p. 197; *General Statutes of Connecticut*, Revision 1887, p. 725.

Warning Out in New England

the town or by residing four years continuously in the town without themselves or their family becoming chargeable to the town during that time.*

The action of Connecticut towns in regard to receiving or warning out new-comers is illustrated by the following instances:—

In the town of Hartford, on the 1st of January, 1638, it was agreed that the selectmen should have power to "order the Comon occations of the Towne," except in certain matters, one of which was that "they receaue noe new Inhabetant into the Towne wthout Aprobacon of the body."†

At a town meeting on February 14, 1659, it was provided that

> For the p^{r}uenting of future euills and inconueniances that many Times are Redy to break in upon us by many P^{r}sons vsshering in themselues among us who are strangers to us, through whose pouerty euill maners or opions the towne is subject to be much p^{r}iudisshed and indamiadged.
>
> It is therefore ordered at the same towne metting that noe p^{r}son or p^{r}sons In Hartford shall giue entertainement or Receiue any fammily p^{r}son or p^{r}sons that is not an Inhabitant soe as to Rent any part of his or thair house to him or them wherby he or thaye becom an inmate, without it bee first Concented to by the orderly uoat of the Inhabitanc at some towne metting vnder the forfiture of fiue pounds for euery month to bee Recouered by the townsmen in being by a cours of law if other means will not p^{r}uaile and this for the use of the towne: & allso all such p^{r}sons as break this order shall be liabl to be called to an acount by the towne and beare all Just damiadges that shall accru to ye towne therby.‡

August 20, 1660, the town of Hartford by their vote "gaue Jarrad Spencer liberty to dwell amongst us as an

---

* *General Statutes of Connecticut*, Sects. 2466, 2469.

† *Hartford Town Votes*, Vol. I, 1635–1716, p. 2, in Connecticut Historical Society Collection, Vol. VI.

‡ *Ibid.*, p. 128, in Connecticut Historical Society Collection, Vol. VI.

inhabitant wth us at Hartford." And at a town meeting held on November 20, 1660,

Y^e Towne by their vote voted that Jeams Blore should not continue wi^{th} us as an Inhabitant:

but upon John Stedmans request they granted him liberty to continnue In Hartford till springe he ye s^d John Stedman engageing to secure ye Town from all damage thereby:

at ye same Town meeting ye Town by there vote did refuse to graunt Thomas marten liberty to be an Inhabitant in Hartford.*

In Guilford the first settlers had a rule that no man should sell or purchase land in the town without leave of the town.†

In Haddam in 1673

It was agreed by voate that John Sled and his wief should not be entertained in the towne as inhabitants or resedence, and also Goodman Corbee was forewarned not to reseave him into his hows becose they weare not persones qualified according to Law.‡

In Enfield in 1683 the first settlers ordered that the inhabitants admitted should continue to live in the town for seven years before "they shall have wright to sell or any ways pass away any of their alotments to any person whatsoever."§

In Wallingford applications for permission to live in the town were presented in town meeting and referred to a committee, which examined the testimonials presented by the applicant as to his character. These testimonials required proof of the good conversation of the persons in the places where they formerly lived, and in 1671 it was ordered that no one should come to dwell as planters in the town

* *Hartford Town Votes,* Vol. I, p. 132, in Connecticut Historical Society Collection, Vol. VI.

† Smith, *History of Guilford,* p. 54.

‡ *The Two Hundredth Anniversary of the First Congregational Church of Haddam, Connecticut,* October 14 and 17, 1900, p. 35.

§ Allen, *History of Enfield,* p. 62.

Warning Out in New England 85

without consent and allowance of the committee of the town "whether they come in by purchase or otherwise."

No sale could be made of any land to a stranger by an inhabitant of the town until the character of the proposed purchaser had been examined and approved, and leave granted by express vote of the town. There are many entries upon the town records like these:—

12th Feb. 1671. Agreed by y^e Comitee for y^e Towne of Wallingford that Isack Rise, and Nehimia Rise, shall have lotts granted y^m provided they procure suficient testamoney of theyr good conversation in the place whear they formerly lived.

20th Oct. 1674 voted that $Good^n$ Foote shall have liberty to buy the lott, y^t is Joseph Eives provided he procure sufficient teastimony of his good conversation in y^e plase wheare he now pretendeth to remove.

Next January, we find "the teastimony for Goo^n foote being sevesente and axepted, he was admited a planter upon the lot that was Joseph eives." 23rd February 1677. The towne gave liberty to Nath'l Hickock to sell his accommodation to any such men as ye towne shall approve of.

December 20, 1679, The towne received Joe Brooks a planter of ye loer Ranks provided he bring sufficient testimony of his good conversation in ye place wheare he formerly lived.

The town also required that persons coming into town temporarily must obtain permission. There are many records of this kind:—

Sep. 1678. The towne gave liberty to Isack Curtice to abide in the town as a sojourner.

Curtice lived in Hartford, and desired to visit his son in Wallingford, who was one of the first citizens of the town.*

In Windsor a similar practice prevailed. The records show that December 1, 1651, "John Moses had

* Davis, *History of Wallingford*, pp. 82, 83, 84, *et seq.*

allowance to sojourn with Simon Miller in his house." Also that "John Bennett should be entertained by William Hayden in his family."

December 10, 1659, the townsmen approved of that Thomas Gunn should entertain as a tabler Capt. Thomas in his family for this winter.

June 27, 1659, it was ordered that

No person or persons whatsoever shall be admitted inhabitant in this town of Windsor without the approbation of the town or townsmen that are or shall be from year to year in being. Nor shall any man sett or sell any house or land so as to bring in any to be inhabitant into the town without the approbation of the townsmen or giving any such security as may be accepted to save the town from damage.

In April, 1699, a widow by the name of Rix made application for liberty to remain in town. The request was not granted, and the record shows that

the townsmen do not see reason to grant her request, but have now warned her to remove out of this town to the town from whence she came or to some other place that she may prevent the townsmen proceeding against her according to law.*

In Woodbury the fundamental articles of agreement signed by the first settlers provided that none of them should sell or let any of their lands or houses to any person but such as the town should approve of, the town promising either to purchase of the persons removing and desiring to sell, or to approve "of such blameless man in his conversation with certificates according to law that shall be presented to buy ye same."†

In New Haven no one was admitted to be a planter or an inhabitant without the consent of the town.

---

* Stiles, *History of Ancient Windsor*, pp. 81, 82.

† Cothren, *History of Ancient Woodbury*, Vol. I, p. 40.

Warning Out in New England 87

May, 1650, a law was passed forbidding the "disposal of any house, house-lott, land, or any part or parcel of the same, to Strangers," and no one was permitted to entertain a stranger longer than three weeks without permission from the authorities.

In 1655, however, by what was known as "Eaton's Code," it was provided that residence within a plantation for a year even without a license was sufficient to cause a stranger to become an inhabitant.

The same custom of admitting inhabitants upon surety to save the town from liability prevailed in Connecticut as in Massachusetts. In 1656 Mrs. Finch, of West Chester, came to New Haven and rented a house, in order that her lame child might be treated by John Winthrop, who was skilled as a surgeon. The town, however, voted not to let her stay unless some approved person offered himself as her security, which being done by two persons, she was permitted to remain.

And when in 1659 John Winthrop, who was then governor of the colony, wished to let his house and lot in New Haven, the town refused to allow it, and forced him to sell it to the town.*

* Livermore, *The Republic of New Haven*, pp. 103, 104, 106.

CHAPTER V.

New Hampshire Colony and State Laws.—Action of Towns as to Inhabitancy, Warning Out, Relief of the Poor, etc.

The first settlers of New Hampshire asserted the right of towns to admit or exclude new-comers. In 1641 the inhabitants of Exeter provided that "none but inhabitants of the town shall plant [settle] within the town's liberties [grant] without their consent." *

The right of towns to exclude strangers was recognized by the "Generall Lawes & Liberties of the Province of New Hampshire made by the Generall Assembly in Portsm°. the 16th of March, $16\frac{79}{80}$ and aproved by the Presid^t and Councill" in these words:—

> Likewise it is further ordered y^t if any pson come into my house wthin this province & be there recd. & entertained 3 m^{oths} if such pson fall sick or lame he shall be relieved by y^t towne where he was soe long entertained but if ye constable of y^t towne or any of ye selectmen have given warning to such pson wthin ye space of 3 m^{oths} y^t ye towne will not admit of him if such pson shall stand in need of reliefe ye towne shall supply his necessity untill ye Presid^t & Coun^{ll} can dispose of him as to y^m shall seem most just and equall.†

Here the necessity for warning out to prevent the town from becoming chargeable for the support of a stranger is clearly recognized.

Two other orders passed at the same time and a part of the so-called Laws and Liberties adopted at Portsmouth October 11, $16\frac{80}{81}$, were as follows:—

> (41) It is also ordered; That if any children, or elder persons shal be sent or come from one Town to another, to School, or

---

* *Laws of New Hampshire, Province Period*, Vol. I, p. 742.
† *Ibid.*, Vol. I, p. 36.

Warning Out in New England 89

to nurs, or otherwise to be educated; or to a Physitian or Surgeon, to be cured or healed; if such shal stand in need of relief, they shal be releeved at the charge of the Town, from whence they came, or do belong; and not by the Town, to which they are sent. AND in case they be sent from any Town without this Province, the taker, nurs, physitian, or surgeon, to whom they are sent, shal take good security to save the Town & Province chargeless, or shal be responsible themselves for such as need releef.*

(43) BE IT also Enacted; THAT no person Master of any Vessel, or other, do bring into any of our Towns within the Province, any person or persons, without the approbation of the President, or three of the Councel, or the Select-men of each Town: Nor that any Inhabitant within this Province, do entertain in his family any person that is not so allowed, for more than one week, without giving notice thereof to one of the Members of the Councel, or to the Select-men of the Town to which they belong; On penalty of forfeiting ffive pound to the Town & of being liable to be sued, & giving bond to free the Town from damage. PROVIDED, this Order shal not hinder any man from taking of an Apprentice, or covenant servant for year or years, that is at pr'sent sound & wel. And if such servant shal fal sick, or lame, He shal be maintained by his Master during the date of his indenture, or coven't and afterwards by the Town in case of necessity.†

In 1718 another Act was passed, entitled "An Act directing the admission of Town inhabitants." The preamble of this Act was as follows:—

For the better preventing of persons obtruding themselves on any particular town within this province, without orderly admission by the inhabitants of such town, or the select-men thereof in manner as hereafter is expressed: and for remedying the manifold inconveniences, and great charge heretofore occasioned thereby: to the intent also, that the select-men may the

---

* *Laws of New Hampshire, Province Period*, Vol. I, § 41, p. 36 (Acts of the Assembly in Portsmouth, October 11, 1680–81).

† *Ibid.*, § 43, p. 37 (Acts of the Assembly in Portsmouth, October 11, 1680–81).

more easily come to the certain knowledge of persons, and their circumstances, that come to reside, and sojourn in such town.

The Act required masters of ships arriving from any other country to give lists of passengers to the naval officer, and, if any passenger should be impotent, lame, or otherwise infirm, or likely to be a charge to the place, and could not give security for saving the town from such charge, the master of the ship should be required to carry him or her out of the province within two months, or give sufficient security to indemnify and keep the town free from charge. The Act then provided as follows:—

That from and after the publication of this act, no person whatever coming to reside or dwell in any town in this province, other than freeholders and proprietors of land in such town, or those born, or that have served an apprenticeship there, and have not remov'd and become inhabitants elsewhere, shall be admitted to the privilege of elections in such towns (though otherwise qualified) unless such person shall first make known his desire to the selectmen thereof, and obtain their approbation, or the approbation of the town, for his dwelling there.

Nor shall any town be obliged to be at charge for the relief and support of any person residing in such town, in case he or she stand in need, that are not approved as aforesaid, unless such person or persons have continued their residence there, by the space of twelve months next before, and have not been warned in manner as the law directs, to depart and leave the town: any law, usage or custom to the contrary notwithstanding.

And if any person orderly warned to depart from any town whereof he or she is not an inhabitant, and being sent by warrant from a justice of peace unto the town whereto such person properly belongs, or to the place of his or her last abode, shall presume to return back, and obtrude him or herself upon the town so sent from, by residing there, every person so offending, shall be proceeded against as a vagabond.*

In 1719 an Act was passed for regulating town-

---

* *Acts and Laws of Province of New Hampshire in New England*, edition 1771, p. 123.

ships, choice of town officers, and setting forth their power, which provided that

> If any person or persons come to sojourn, or dwell in any town within this province, or precinct thereof, and be there received, and entertained by the space of three months, not having been warned by the constable, or other person whom the select-men shall appoint for that end to leave the place, and the names of such persons with the time of their abode there, and when such warning was given them, returned unto the court of quarter sessions; every such person shall be reputed an inhabitant of such town, or precinct of the same, and the proper charge of the same, in case, through sickness, lameness, or otherwise, they come to stand in need of relief, to be born by such town; unless the relations of such poor impotent persons in the line of father, or grand-father, mother, or grand-mother, children, or grand-children be of sufficient ability; then such relations respectively shall relieve such poor person in such manner as the justices of the peace shall assess, on pain that every one failing therein, shall forfeit thirty shillings for every months neglect, to be levied by distress and sale of such offenders goods, by warrant from any two justices of the peace, *unus quorum*, within this province. *Provided nevertheless*, this act shall not be understood of any person committed to prison, or lawfully restrained in any town, or of such as shall come, or be sent for nursing, or education, or to any phycisian, or chyrurgeon, to be healed or cured, but the particular persons who receive and entertain any such shall be the towns security in their behalf, and be obliged to relieve and support them, in case of need, upon complaint made to the quarter sessions, who shall accordingly order the same.
>
> And it is further enacted by the authority aforesaid, that any person, orderly warned, as aforesaid, to depart any town where he is not an inhabitant, and neglecting so to do by the space of fourteen days next after such warning given, may by warrant from the next justice of the peace be sent and conveyed from constable to constable, unto the town where he properly belongs, or had his last residence at his own charge, if able to pay the same, or otherwise at the charge of the town so sending him.*

---

* *Acts and Laws of Province of New Hampshire in New England*, edition 1771, pp. 136, 140.

In 1766 an Act was passed in addition to the Act of 1719 directing the admission of town inhabitants, imposing a penalty for entertaining strangers, and providing that the expense of warning such persons as were not inhabitants should be defrayed by the persons who entertained them, as follows:—

Whereas the said act has not sufficiently provided against persons secretly entertaining strangers in their houses till they become inhabitants, which by another law of this province they are allowed to be in three months, by which means many persons become inhabitants of towns, before they are known to live in the town, by the officers whose care it is to take notice of such matters, for remedy whereof

BE IT ENACTED BY THE GOVERNOR COUNCIL AND ASSEMBLY, that the inhabitants of the several towns within this province and parishes having the privileges of towns, who shall receive admit and entertain any person or persons not being inhabitants of such towns or parishes, either as inmates, boarders or tenants in the house where such person dwells, or in any other house whatsoever within this province, or under any other qualifications whatsoever, for more than the space of twenty days and shall not in writing under their hands give an account to one or more of the select-men, or the town clerk of such town of all such person or persons so received, admitted or entertained by them, with the time they first received them and the place from whence they last came, together with their circumstances as far as they can, shall for every such neglect forfeit & pay the sum of twenty shillings to be recovered by bill plaint or information before any justice of the peace or in any of his majesty's courts of record within this province, the one half of the said fine to be employed to and for the use of the poor of the town or parish where such officers shall be committed the other half to him or them that shall inform and sue for the same & they shall be liable to answer all charges that may arise in said town or parish by receiving & entertaining such person or persons as aforesaid, to be recovered by the town treasurer or select-men where no treasurer is appointed, who are hereby respectively impowered to bring an action accordingly.

And be it further enacted that all costs and charges arising by warning any such persons as are not inhabitants entering the caution or carrying them out of town, shall be defrey'd and pay'd by those who received & entertained such person or persons in their houses as aforesaid and shall be recovered as afores^d for the uses afores^d, & the town treasurer or select-men afores^d, are hereby directed and ordered, before they bring their action to exhibit to such who receive and entertain any person or persons in their houses as afores^d an acco^t of the charges arising thereby and upon refusing to pay the same within five days they shall be liable to pay said charges and be deprived of their benefit by their notification tho' given within the twenty days as afores^d, [this act to continue and be in force for the term of five years and no longer.]*

In 1771 an Act was passed providing that the time within which warning out would defeat a settlement be extended to twelve months, as follows:—

WHEREAS in and by an act or law of this province made and passed in the fifth year of the reign of King George the First it is among other things enacted that if any person or persons come to sojourn or dwell in any town within this province or precinct thereof, and be there received and entertained by the space of three months, not having been warned by the constable or other person whom the select-men shall appoint for that end, to leave the place and the names of such persons with the time of their abode there, & when such warning was given them returned unto the court of general sessions of the peace; every such person shall be reputed an inhabitant of such town or precinct of the same, to be relieved by such town in case of need—which time or space of three months is found to be too short for the purposes aforesaid, the select-men in many instances not being able to discover such poor person or persons within that time. For remedy whereof

Be it enacted by the governor, council and assembly that from and after the first day of july next no person or persons shall gain a settlement in any town or parish within this province by dwelling therein without being warned out according to law: For any term of time less than one year.

*Acts and Laws of Province of New Hampshire in New England, edition 1771, Appendix, p. 25.

April 9, 1777, this Act was revived and re-enacted by the State of New Hampshire by "An Act for the re-establishing the general system of laws heretofore in force in this State."*

February 15, 1791, in "An Act for the punishment of idle and disorderly persons, for the support and maintenance of the poor, and for designating the duties and defining the powers of overseers of the poor," it was provided among other things that

> Every person who hath lived one year in any town or place, shall be deemed an inhabitant of such town or place, unless some time within such year, and before the expiration thereof, such person shall have been by warrant from the selectmen of such town or place directed to any constable thereof (or other person to whom they may think proper to direct the same) warned to depart from such town or place, and the said warrant and the return of such warning made by the person to whom directed, within the time aforesaid, returned to the clerk of the court of general sessions of the peace in the same county, and put on file, which shall always be done by the said clerk, and a minute thereon made of the time of receiving the same. And the said clerk shall receive six pence therefor. Provided always, That nothing in this section contained, shall be construed to extend to persons committed, or lawfully restrained in any town, or to such as shall be sent for education, or to any physician to be healed or cured.

Then followed a provision that the taxing or assessing of any person (warned to depart) for such lands, property, and ratable estate as he might have used, occupied, or possessed, during his residence in such town, should not be considered or construed as entitling the person so taxed or assessed to the rights and privileges of an inhabitant, or operate in any wise to "injure or lessen the full force, validity and effect of such warning."†

---

* *Perpetual Laws of New Hampshire*, Melcher's edition, 1789, p. 160.

† *New Hampshire Laws*, 1792, Melcher's edition, p. 304. See also *New Hampshire Laws*, 1805, p. 300.

Warning Out in New England 95

On December 20, 1797, an Act was passed with regard to the removal of persons of vicious character having no visible means of support and no settlement. This provided that such persons might by warrant from the selectmen directed to a constable be warned to depart from a town or place, and, if they neglected to do so for the space of fourteen days after warning, they might be carried to the town or place in which they were last settled. And, if any person so removed should voluntarily return to the town from which they were first carried and remain seven days, they might be apprehended by order of a justice, and on conviction the justice might "sentence him or her to be publicly whipped, not exceeding ten stripes." The form of warning was set forth in the statute, and stated that the person was "of vicious character, or has no visible means of support,"* as the case may be.

This Act, it will be observed, made a distinction between persons who were merely warned to depart to prevent their obtaining a settlement and those who were of vicious character or had no visible means of support.

The practice under these Acts is shown by the following cases:—

In Littleton it was the practice to warn out the newcomers, whether desirable persons or not. This record shows the form of procedure:—

STATE of NEW HAMPSHIRE ⎱ To LEVI ALDRICH Constable of
GRAFTON ss ⎰ the town of Littleton *Greeting.*

In the name of the State You are Required to go forthwith to the house of Samuel Underwood now residing in this town and warn the following persons (viz.) Samuel Underwood, Beulah

* *New Hampshire Laws,* 1805, p. 306.

Underwood, Junior Israel Underwood to Depart out of Town (as they came in without leave) and Trespass no more in said Town. Given under our hands this 29th day of August 1769.

> ROBERT CHARLTON
> EBEN PINGREE } Selectmen.
> ANSAL HATCH

In Henniker all persons coming into town were warned to depart within a specified time. It is said, however, that but little attention was paid to the warning, and in most cases it was hoped there would be no attention paid to it. Occasionally, however, persons took the matter seriously and left the town.*

In Peterboro warning out was practised against all new-comers. The town record shows that December 23, 1763, a warning was issued and served, as follows:—

PROVINCE OF }
NEW HAMPSHIRE }   December ye 23d 1763

To James Templeton Constable of this town of Peterborough in His Majesty's name, we command you forthwith warn Jean Culberson now in this place forthwith to Depart out of this town, hereof fail not as you will answer the Contrary At yr Perill. Thomas Cunningham Alexr Robbe Hugh Gregg Selectmen, etc.

December ye 24th 1763, according to the within request, I have Warned Jean Culberson forthwith to depart out of this town etc.

James Templeton, Constable for the Town of Peterborough.†

In Rindge warning out was practised as early as January, 1769, the warrant of warning being issued before the Revolution in his Majesty's name and served and recorded upon the town books.

On June 12, 1776, the town records show that £2 13s. 4d. were paid to a constable of the town "for warning forty persons out of the town," and that in October

---

* Cogswell, *History of Henniker*, p. 342.
† Smith, *History of Peterboro*, p. 176.

Warning Out in New England 97

of the same year 10s. 8d. was paid for warning eight persons out of the town. In 1772 and 1773 fifty-nine persons were warned out by Constable Jonathan Parker, Jr. The learned historian of the town, Ezra S. Stearns, says that many of the persons who were warned to depart became prosperous in business, honored as townsmen, and their descendants have been useful and esteemed citizens.*

In Antrim, beginning in 1783, warning out was practised generally, a warrant from the selectmen directed to the persons ordered to depart being served by constable and returned and recorded upon the town records. The historian of the town alludes to this custom as a curiosity at the present time, and says that notwithstanding the warning the parties might remain, and generally were desired to remain, only, in case they became a public charge, the town where they had resided was held for their support. And then he adds, "Happily this law has long since passed away."†

In Exeter it was ordered in 1665 that all persons who should hire any servant should be chargeable for his support "if it happened that he should be lamed or any way unserviceable made in work during the time for which he was hired, so the town may be free from such charges."

In August, 1671, it was ordered

> That no man shall receive any person or persons into town without the consent of the Selectmen, or security to free the town from any charge that may ensue thereby, upon twenty shillings a month forfeiture; and that no man shall come to inhabit, by purchase or otherwise, without the consent of the Selectmen upon the same penalty.‡

---
* Stearns, *History of Rindge*, p. 88 et seq.
† Cochrane, *History of Antrim, N.H.*, p. 68.
‡ Bell, *History of Exeter*, p. 54.

In Walpole, in 1772, the town voted

That the constable warn out of town every person that comes in that has no estate in town.

And this was made one of the duties of the constable for many years thereafter.*

The same practice was followed in Alstead and many other towns, especially after the Revolutionary War, when many persons came to dwell in the new towns in the Connecticut Valley and in the northern part of the State.

* Aldrich, *History of Walpole*, p. 43.

CHAPTER VI.

RHODE ISLAND COLONY AND STATE LAWS AS TO INHABITANCY, RELIEF OF THE POOR, TOWN SETTLEMENT, ETC.—MAINE AND VERMONT STATE LAWS AS TO WARNING OUT, INHABITANCY, SETTLEMENT, RELIEF OF THE POOR, ETC.

The early settlers in Rhode Island asserted the same right to exclude new-comers. When Roger Williams in 1638 conveyed to twelve of his companions the land which had been conveyed to him by the Indian chiefs Cononicus and Miontinomi, on the Pawtuxet River, the grant was to share with him "and such others as the major part of us shall admit into the same fellowship of vote with us."

The subsequent compact for the establishment of the town of Providence was upon the same principle. It was as follows:—

We whose names are hereunder, desirous to inhabit in the town of Providence, do promise to subject ourselves in active or passive obedience to all such orders or agreements as shall be made for public good of the body, in an orderly way by the major assent of the present inhabitants, masters of families, incorporated together into a town fellowship, and such others as they shall admit unto them, only in civil things.*

The same method was followed in the settlement of Aquidneck, Rhode Island, in 1638. In the town compact made in 1640 five men were appointed to dispose of the town lands, but they were required first to notify the inhabitants lest any objection should exist to the new-comer, and any inhabitant could object and require the question of admitting the stranger to be determined by a town meeting.

Conveyances were made in simple form without the

* Arnold, *History of Rhode Island*, Vol. I, pp. 100, 103.

voluminous provisions of recitals and covenants, etc., in modern deeds of land, and were read in an open town meeting, and were valid only when approved by vote of the meeting.*

It was agreed in the form of government at Providence the 27th of the 5th mo. in the yeare (so called) 1640 (1637) in the second statement as follows:—

We have with one consent agreed that for the disposeing, of those lands that shall be disposed belonging to this towne of Providence to be in the whole Inhabitants by the choise of five men for generall disposeall, to be betrusted with disposeall of lands and also of the townes Stocke, and all Generall things and not to receive in any six dayes as townesmen, but first to give the Inhabitants notice to consider if any have just cause to shew against the receiving of him as you can apprehend, and to receive none but such as subscribe to this our determination. Also, we agree that if any of our neighbours doe apprehend himselfe wronged by these or any of these 5 disposers, that at the Generall towne meeting he may have a tryall.†

At a generall meeting of the town of Portsmouth "upon publicke notice on the 3d month, 13 day, 1638," it was

Ordered, that none shall be received as inhabitants or Freemen, to build or plant upon the Island but such as shall be received in by the consent of the Bodye, and do submit to the Government that is or shall be established, according to the word of God.‡

At the Generall Court assembled at Newport on the 19th of September, 1642, it was

Ordered, that no person or persons shall make any sale of his lands (in or belonging to our Jurisdiction) to any other Jurisdiction, or person therein, vnless that that Jurisdiction or person shall be subject to the Government here established, vpon paine of forfeiture of the said lands so proffered.§

* Arnold, *History of Rhode Island*, Vol. I, pp. 9, 121, 127.
† *Rhode Island Colony Records*, 1636 to 1663, Vol. I, p. 28.
‡ *Ibid.*, p. 53.
§ *Ibid.*, p. 126.

Warning Out in New England 101

One of the acts and orders made and agreed upon at the General Court of Election in Rhode Island, on the 19th, 20th, and 21st of May, 1647, for the Colony and Province of Providence, was:—

> It is agreed and ordered, by this present Assembly, that each Towne shall provide carefully for the reliefe of the poore, to maintayne the impotent, and to employ the able, and shall appoint an overseer for the same purpose. See 43 Eliz. 2.*

In 1682 it was provided by law that the town council could prevent any one becoming an inhabitant unless sufficient security satisfactory to them was given by townsmen that the person admitted should not become a public charge. In the Laws of Rhode Island of 1798 "An Act providing for the Relief, Support, Employment and Removal of the Poor" provided that:—

> Every town in this State shall be holden to relieve and support all poor and indigent persons, lawfully settled therein, whenever they shall stand in need thereof.†

Section 15 of this Act provided:—

> That in case any tavern-keeper, inn-holder, victualler, or any other person whosoever, inhabiting in any town within this State, shall entertain or keep in his or her house any single person or family, being strangers, for more than one whole week from the time of their coming into such town, without giving notice thereof in writing to the President of the Town-Council, such person so offending shall forfeit and pay a fine of seven dollars for every such offence, to be recovered by the Town-Treasurer of such town, before any Justice or Warden, to and for the use of such town.

As late as 1727 the town councils had by statute power to refuse inhabitancy to any stranger, even if security was given.‡

In that portion of Massachusetts, now the State of

---

* *Records of the Colony of Rhode Island*, 1636–1663, Vol. I, pp. 184, 185.
† See *Rhode Island Laws*, 1727, 1741, 1748, 1765, 1798.
‡ Stokes, *The Finances and Administration of Providence*, p. 74.

Maine, then commonly known as the District of Maine, warning out was practised until the State of Maine was created in 1819. The following instances illustrate the practice:—

In Sanford, incorporated in 1768, warning out began to be practised as early as 1771, and appears to have been used against all new-comers. The first warrant was as follows:—

York ∫s   Sanford June ye 28: 1771.

Paletiah Tingle Wereas you have come into this Towne Withoute Leav of the Towne This is to warne you forthwith to Departe out of this Towne forthwith for Wee Disowne you for an inhabitant.*

In Belfast, incorporated in 1773, new-comers were warned out as early as 1775, and the practice was continued as late as 1798.†

In Gorham warning out was practised as early as 1791, a warning being then recorded warning out fourteen persons with their families "who have lately come into this towne for the purpose of abiding therein not having obtained the towns consent therefor."‡

In Union in 1787 it was voted that the selectmen should warn out all persons they might deem it necessary to warn, and in December of the same year and in 1789 warning out warrants were issued and served upon sundry new-comers.§

In Thomaston in 1785 seventeen persons were warned out, including, as it afterwards proved, many who became valuable and thrifty citizens. It is said by Eaton that the practice of warning out became gen-

* Emery, *History of Sanford*, p. 225.
† Williamson, *History of Belfast*, p. 133.
‡ McLellan, *History of Gorham*, p. 334.
§ Sibley, *History of Union*, pp. 270, 271.

eral throughout the State toward all new-comers without discrimination.*

In Camden the selectmen were authorized to warn out all new-comers who had not been admitted by the town authorities to be inhabitants. The record shows that January 2, 1792, twenty-two persons were thus warned out of town. Among the number were several who afterwards became among the first citizens of the town.†

In Castine one of the first acts of the town, after its incorporation in 1796, was to warn a woman to depart, and a few weeks later to warn out five other persons. These are said to have been the only cases of warning out in Castine, which was created from a portion of the town of Penobscot, but the records of Penobscot show that warning out was practised there. In 1790 fifty persons were warned to depart the town.‡

In Durham, incorporated 1789, the town at once began to warn out all new-comers, and continued the practice for some time. Three persons were warned out in 1791, but remained and were good citizens. The following from the town records of 1793 illustrates the course of procedure:—

Cumberland Ss to Benjamin Vining Constable for the said Town of Durham . . . . GREETING You are in the name of the Commonwealth of Massachusetts directed To warn, and give notice unto Samuel Jordan, Jedediah Jordan, Daniel Roberson, Paul Dyer of Cape Elizabeth . . . John Stackpole, Jeremiah Smith, James Johnson of Harpswell, Daniel Harmon of Standish, Elias Davis of Bakerstown, Ezekiel Turner of Freeport, and Samuel Proctor of Plymouth Labourers in the Town of Durham and County of Cumberland,

---

* Eaton, *History of Thomaston*, p. 172.

† *Camden Town Records*, pp. 22, 28, 39, cited by Locke, *History of Camden*, p. 69.

‡ Wheeler, *History of Castine*, pp. 69, 74.

Which above named persons, has lately come into this Town for the Purpose of abiding therein, not having obtained the Towns consent. Therefore that they depart the Limits thereof, With their Children And others under their care, if any they have, within fifteen days. And of this precept, with your doings thereon, you are to make Return into the office of the Town, within Twenty days next Coming, that such further proceedings may be had in the premises, As the law directs. . . . Given under our hands and Seal, at Durham aforesaid this 25 day of February A.D. 1793.

NATHANIEL GARISH } Select
AARON OSGOOD } men
Attest   MARTIN ROURK, Town Clerk

Pursuant to the within Warrant, I have warned those persons within mentioned To Depart the Limits of the Town As soon as may be, or within fifteen days, from the date thereof.

  BENJAMIN VINING   Constable
A true copy   MARTIN ROURK   T Clerk
Durham, March ye 14, 1793.*

This warning out of all new-comers is probably to be accounted for by the fact that there was much immigration into the new and poor towns at that time.

One provision of the Constitution of Maine, adopted October 29, 1819, was that all laws then in force, not repugnant to the Constitution then adopted, should remain in force until altered or repealed by the Legislature, or until they should expire by their own limitation.†

In 1821 a Settlement Act was passed, differing somewhat from the Massachusetts Act. It did not provide for warning out in any form, and, as the Massachusetts law did not then provide for warning, there was never any statute providing for warning out in

---

* Stackpole, *History of Durham*, p. 24.
† Constitution of Maine, Article 10, Section 3.

the State of Maine. The Act of 1821 omitted the provision in the Massachusetts Act for the settlement of settled and ordained ministers, but provided that a person could be admitted an inhabitant of any town at a town meeting the warrant for which contained an article for that purpose. The further provisions of the Act were in substance:—

1. That all persons dwelling and having their homes in any unincorporated places, when the same should be incorporated into a town, should thereby gain a legal settlement in the town.

2. That legal settlements, in case of new towns or division of towns, should be in the new town within the boundaries of which the persons actually dwelt and had their homes.

3. That any minor who should serve an apprenticeship to any lawful trade for four years in any town, and actually set up his trade therein within one year after the expiration of such four years, and was then twenty-one years of age, should thereby have a settlement in such town.

4. That any person twenty-one years of age, who should reside in any town for five years together, and not during that time, directly or indirectly, receive supplies or support as a pauper from any town, should gain a settlement.

5. That any person resident in a town at the date of the passage of the Act, who should not within one year previous to that date have received support or supplies from some town as a pauper, should be deemed to have a settlement in the town where he then dwelt and had his home.

The Act also declared that every legal settlement when gained should continue until lost or defeated by gaining a new one, and that, upon gaining such new settlement, all former settlements should be defeated and lost.*

In Vermont, which was an independent State until 1791, the right of towns to exclude strangers was recognized and established in 1787 by the following Act of the General Assembly:—

AN ACT for the ordering and disposing of transient persons.

Be it enacted, and it is hereby enacted, by the representatives of the freemen of the State of Vermont, in General Assembly met, and by the authority of the same, that the select-men of each respective town in this State, shall be, and are hereby, authorised and impowered to warn any transient person (residing in such town, that is not of a quiet and peaceable behaviour, or is, in their opinion, like to be chargable to such town) to depart out of such town, except such person does obtain a vote of the inhabitants of such town, in legal town meeting, to remain in such town; and if any such person or persons, being so warned, do not leave such town within twenty days after such warning, then one or more of said select-men may make application to an assistant or justice of the peace, who is hereby impowered to issue his warrant to the sheriff or constable to take such person or persons, and transport him or them to the next town, towards the place where such person was last an inhabitant;—in the same manner to be transported to the place where such person or persons were inhabitants last, or in the same way, out of this State, if he be not an inhabitant thereof; and all such expence shall be paid by the person or persons so warned, if of ability, but if he is not of ability, to be paid by such town.

PROVIDED ALWAYS, that no person shall be subject to such warning, after he or she has lived in such town one year.

BE IT FURTHER ENACTED, BY THE AUTHORITY AFORESAID, that if any transient person or persons shall be taken sick or lame, in any town in this State; whoever shall keep any such person or persons (if such transient, sick or lame person or persons be not of sufficient ability) shall defray all such expense, until complaint thereof be by him made to the select-men of such town; after

---

* *Laws of the State of Maine,* 1821, Chap. 122.

which, such select-men shall provide for such transient, sick, or lame person, according to law.*

At the same session an Act was passed for maintaining and supporting the poor. This Act first provided "that each town in this State shall take care of, support, and maintain their own poor."

And the Act also provided

that if any person or persons shall come to live in any town in this State, and be there received and entertained, by the space of twelve months; and if, by sickness, lameness, or the like, he or they come to want relief, every such person or persons shall be provided for by that town wherein he or they were so long entertained, at said town's own proper cost and charge, unless such person or persons by law are to be provided for by some particular person or persons; or unless such person or persons wanting relief, have, within the said twelve months, been warned as the law directs, to depart and leave the place: and if such warning be given, and the same be certified to the next superior court to be held in the same county, the said court shall and may otherwise order the defraying the charge arising about such indigent person or persons.†

March 9, 1787, an Act was passed entitled "An Act providing for and ordering transient, idle, impotent and poor persons."

This Act provided "that each town in this State shall take care of, support and maintain its own poor."

And also provided

"that no persons shall gain a settlement in any town in this State, and be liable to be supported thereby, unless such person was born therein, or has owned or shall own estate in such town of the value of two hundred pounds clear of all demands against him, or her, or of the yearly value of ten pounds." ‡

March 3, 1797, an Act was passed "defining what shall be deemed and adjudged a legal settlement, and

---

* *Vermont Laws*, February, 1779. *Vermont State Papers*, p. 315.
† *Vermont State Papers*, pp. 378, 379.
‡ *Statutes of Vermont*, edition 1791.

for the support of the poor," etc., indexed under the head of "Inhabitancy."

The first section of that Act provided for obtaining settlement as follows:—

> Section 1. It is hereby enacted by the General Assembly of the State of Vermont, That every person who shall purchase a freehold estate of the value of one hundred dollars, and shall have bona fide paid therefor, and shall actually occupy and improve the same for the term of one whole year; or shall actually and bona fide have rented and occupied a tenement of the yearly value of twenty dollars or upwards, for the term of two whole years, and actually paid such rent; and every person who shall inhabit in any town or place within this state, and shall for himself, or on his own account, have executed any public office or charge in such town or place, during one whole year, or shall have been charged with and paid his or her share of the public rates or taxes of such town or place for the space of two years; and every person who shall have been bound an apprentice or servant by indenture, or by any deed, contract or writing not indented, and shall in consequence of such binding, have served a term not less than three years next preceding the time of such apprentice's arriving at the age of twenty-one years, if a male, or at the age of eighteen years, if a female, in such town or place, shall be deemed and adjudged to have attained a legal settlement in such town or place; and every other healthy able bodied person coming and residing within this state, and being of peaceable behaviour, shall be deemed and adjudged to be legally settled in the town or place in which he or she shall have first resided for the space of one whole year; and every bastard child shall be deemed and adjudged to be settled in the town or place of the last legal settlement of his or her mother.

The Act contained provisions for ascertaining by the judgment of two justices of the peace whether new-comers were likely to become chargeable as poor to the town, and, if so, for transporting them out of the town, but it contained no provision authorizing other new-comers to be warned to leave the town.*

* *Laws of Vermont*, 1798, Chap. 18.

Warning Out in New England 109

The first section of this Act was repealed November 6, 1801, by

An act in addition to an act entitled "An act defining what shall be deemed and adjudged a legal Settlement, and for the support of the poor, for designating the duties and powers of the overseers of the poor; and for the punishment of idle and disorderly persons," and for repealing part of the same.

SECTION 1.

It is hereby enacted by the General Assembly of the State of Vermont, That whenever any person, or persons, shall come and reside within any town in this state, the select men of such town, may at their discretion, warn such person, or persons, to depart said town, which warning shall be directed to either constable of said town, and be in the following form, viz.

STATE OF VERMONT.

ss. To either Constable of A. in the county of B. *Greeting.*

You are hereby required to summon C. D. now residing in A. to depart said town. Hereof fail not, but of this precept, and your doings herein, due return make according to law.—Given under our hands, at A. this   day of
A.D. 18

E. F.
G. H. } Select men of A.
I. K.

Which precept shall be served on such person, or persons, coming and residing as aforesaid, by such constable, in the same manner as is provided for the service of writs of summons, in the twenty-sixth section of the act, entitled "An act constituting the supreme and county courts, defining their power, and regulating judicial proceedings"; which precept the said constable shall return, with his proceedings thereon, to the town clerk of such town, within eight days after serving the same, which precept and return it shall be the duty of the town clerk to enter on the records of said town.

SEC. 2. And it is hereby further enacted, That each and every person removing into, and residing within any town in this state, who shall be warned as is prescribed in the preceding section of this act, shall not be deemed and adjudged to have gained a legal settlement in such town, unless such person or persons, is or are discharged from such warning, by a vote of said town, in a legal town meeting warned for said purpose.

SEC. 3. Provided nevertheless, And it is hereby further enacted, That if any person, or persons, removing into, and residing within any town in this state, shall by the inhabitants of such town, be chosen into either of the offices of select men, town clerk, constable, grand juror or lister, and serve the town in such capacity one whole year, he or they shall be considered as gaining a legal settlement in such town, any thing in this act to the contrary notwithstanding.

SEC. 4. And it is hereby further enacted, That all and every person coming into, and residing within any town in this state, who shall not be warned agreeably to the first section of this act, within one year after he or she removes into such town, shall be deemed and adjudged to have attained a legal settlement in such town.

AND WHEREAS difficulties have arisen in procuring two justices of the peace, not inhabitants of the towns concerned, to hear and determine certain causes, and issue certain warrants and orders, as mentioned in the act, to which this is an addition:

THEREFORE,

SEC. 5. It is hereby further enacted, That any two justices of the peace of the county, in which any town lies, which shall take any advantage of said act, shall to all intents and purposes, be competent to hear and determine any cause mentioned in said act, and to issue any warrant or order therein specified, whether they be inhabitants of such town or not, any thing in said act to the contrary notwithstanding.

SEC. 6. And it is hereby further enacted, That if any person who shall be removed from any town in this state, as provided in the third section of the act, to which this is an addition, shall return to reside within the same, without the permission of the select men of such town, and be thereof convicted, he, she or they shall be whipped, not exceeding ten stripes, at the discretion of the justice of the peace before whom such trial shall be had.

SEC. 7. And it is hereby further enacted, That the first section of the act to which this is an addition, be, and the same is hereby repealed.

Passed November 6, 1801.*

* *Acts and Laws of the State of Vermont at their Session at Newbury, in October,* 1801, p. 8.

Warning Out in New England   111

The practice of warning out under these Acts is shown by the following cases:—

In Cornwall it was the custom for many years to serve a summons of warning out upon every newcomer, which was recorded with the officer's returns upon the town books. These warnings cover many pages of the records.*

In Newbury warning out was practised generally with regard to all new-comers. The selectmen issued a warrant, which the constables served and returned, and it was then recorded on the town records. In the first book of town proceedings there are 112 such warnings recorded, the first being January 5, 1787, the last November 12, 1816, when the law authorizing warning out was repealed. One of these warrants includes twenty-four different families.†

In Hartford it was customary to warn out all new-comers, and hundreds of families were thus legally warned to depart. The last warnings were in 1817.‡

Warning out appears to have been most frequently practised in the new towns, probably because there were more new-comers in those towns, and the towns themselves were less able to bear the expense of supporting such persons as might become in need of public support. This was especially the case in those portions of Vermont along the Connecticut River into which a large immigration took place just after the War of the Revolution.

The process of warning out produced three kinds of fees to town officers: first, a fee to the selectmen for making the warrant; second, the fee to the constable

---

* Matthews, *History of Cornwall*, p. 309.

† Wells, *History of Newbury, Vermont*, p. 286.

‡ Tucker, *History of Hartford, Vermont*, p. 305.

for serving the warrant; and, third, a fee to the town clerk for recording the warrant and return of service.*

In Rockingham, which includes Bellows Falls, warnings out were very numerous.

July 24, 1769, it was voted in town meeting that "all Strangers who Com to Inhabit in said town Not being Freeholders, be warned out of town."†

Pages of the town's records are filled by the returns of warrants warning people out of town. The warrants specified the names of all members of the family, sometimes eight or ten in number. One warrant contained the names of fifty persons. In 1808 thirty-one families were warned out, and in 1809 twenty-six.

The warnings of the warrants stated that they were made on complaint made to the selectmen. The last of these warnings was October 10, 1817.

In this town every new-comer, or stranger, was warned out under the vote of the town requiring all persons that "do come into the town to be at once warned out." Of course, few people went because they were warned out. The only effect of the warning was that the persons warned could not afterwards obtain a settlement in the town so as to become chargeable to it for relief, unless they were elected to some town office.‡

The form of warrant used in Rockingham was as follows:—

STATE OF VERMONT, } To either Constable of Rockingham in
WINDHAM COUNTY ss. } the County of Windham *Greeting:*

You are hereby required to summon Samuel March & Tabatha March his Wife & Hannah March Prudence March Abigail March & Sarah March now residing in Rockingham to depart

---

* *History of Newbury, Vermont,* p. 286.
† *History of Rockingham, Vermont,* p. 100 *et seq.*
‡ Thomas B. Peck, *Vital Records of Rockingham, Vermont,* Boston, 1908.

Warning Out in New England

said Town. Hereof fail not but of this precept and your doings thereon doe return make according to law.

Given under our hands at Rockingham this 8th Day of May Anno Domini, 1805.

ELIJAH KNIGHT, } Selectmen
QUARTUS MORGAN, } of
DAVID WOOD, } Rockingham

At Rockingham in the County of Windham this 18th Day of May 1805 I served this summons by leaving a true and attested copy of the same with the within Samuel March's Wife at his Dwelling house in said Rockingham with this my return thereon.

ELIJAH READ, Constable.

On November 4, 1817, an Act was passed prescribing the different ways in which legal settlement could be obtained in a town, and warning out to prevent a settlement ceased. Among other provisions retained in the law, however, was this:—

Any person may be admitted to a legal settlement in any town by vote of the town in a town meeting legally warned and holden for that purpose.*

This provision was embodied in the Laws of Vermont, 1824, page 382, and is found in the Compiled Statutes of Vermont in 1859, p. 128, as follows:—

Any person that shall be admitted an inhabitant by the town at any legal meeting held under a warning, which shall contain an article for that purpose, shall thereby acquire a legal settlement therein.

After the Act of 1817 there was no more warning out in Vermont, but the previous records of such warnings are of much value as fixing the times when the persons warned must have come into the towns.

* *Laws of Vermont*, 1825, Chap. 47, No. 3, p. 381.

CHAPTER VII.

The Length of Time Warning Out was practised.—Effect of Warning Out, how avoided.—Value of Warning Out Records.—Summary as to Reasons for Warning Out, etc.

It will be seen by examination of the statutes and records from which I have made such copious extracts that warning out was practised by the towns in Massachusetts from the early settlement of the colony, first, under the general power of towns to admit or exclude new-comers from inhabitancy, and then under the colony laws until the passage of the Settlement Act in 1793. It was also practised in the Plymouth Colony from the early settlement of that colony until its union with Massachusetts, and was also authorized by the Articles of Confederation between the colonies of Massachusetts, Plymouth, and Connecticut in 1672. The original colony statutes and the Articles of Confederation between the colonies were general in their provisions as to warning out, and did not fix any specific time within which a person should be warned out to prevent his obtaining settlement in a town.

But in 1692 the Massachusetts Bay Colony passed an Act which required persons to be warned out within three months after they came into a town, to prevent their gaining a settlement therein. In 1700 the period within which they might effectively be warned out was extended to twelve months, and this continued to be the period within which a warning must be given to prevent settlement until warning out ceased under the Settlement Act of 1793.

In Connecticut warning out prevailed by custom of

Warning Out in New England 115

towns and by the colony statutes from 1669, and in 1679 it was provided by law that, to be effective against obtaining a settlement, persons should be warned out within three months from the time they came into the town. In 1771 this period was extended to twelve months, which continued to be the period until warning out ceased as to persons living in Connecticut under the Settlement Act of 1796. In New Hampshire warning out was practised by the towns from the early settlement in 1638, and was soon provided for by the colony. In 1679 the period within which persons must be warned out, to prevent obtaining a settlement, was made in three months after they came into the town. In 1771 this period was extended to twelve months, which continued to be the period until the Settlement Act of 1796. In Maine the practice and the statutes for warning out were those of Massachusetts, of which it was a part until 1821. In Vermont warning out was authorized in 1779. The period fixed by the statute within which the warning must be given to prevent a settlement being obtained was fixed at twelve months after the persons came into the town, and this continued to be the limit until warning out ceased under the Settlement Act of 1817.

Warning out, therefore, was practised in some form in Massachusetts for more than one hundred and thirty years, in Maine for more than one hundred years, in Vermont for thirty-eight years, in New Hampshire for one hundred and seventeen years, and in Connecticut for one hundred and twenty-seven years.

In Rhode Island warning out was never authorized by statute, but the right to exclude new-comers from inhabitancy in towns was always exercised in the town councils from the early settlement down to as late certainly as 1727.

The effect of warning out as thus practised upon persons who remained in the town after being warned was to relieve the town from all obligation to aid them if they became poor and in need of help or support. They were inhabitants of the town for all purposes except being helped if they needed help. They paid taxes, they could vote, they could hold office, they could perform all the duties of citizenship and of taxpayers, and yet, if they had been warned out, they could have no help from the town. They might be taxed for the support of others who were in need, but, when they came to be in need, they were entitled to no help from the taxes of the town. They were spoken of among their neighbors as persons who had "been warned." Persons now living remember when those who had been warned out were spoken of in the towns among their neighbors as having "been warned."

The effect of being warned out could be avoided by the election or admission of a person warned as an inhabitant by a vote of the town. In Connecticut it could be avoided, under an Act passed in 1784, by the person warned being "appointed to and executing some public office." In Vermont, by an Act passed in 1801, the effect of warning out could be avoided by the person warned being chosen and serving one whole year in the office of selectman, town clerk, constable, grand juror, or lister. In Massachusetts the effect of warning could also be avoided by the person warned becoming a settled minister in the town.

It has been the law in Massachusetts since 1793 that

> Every settled ordained minister of the gospel shall be deemed to have acquired a legal settlement in the town where he is or may be settled as a minister.

Warning Out in New England 117

The effect of this is that, whenever a man becomes a settled ordained minister of the gospel in a town, he loses any settlement he may previously have had in another town and acquires a settlement in that town. It is not necessary that a minister who has been once regularly ordained in a town, and who afterwards becomes a settled minister in another town, should be again ordained, or that his engagement in the new town should be for any particular time, or that he should be inducted into his ministerial office in the new town by any particular ceremony.*

The town records of these warnings out, and the statutes by which they were authorized, are of much importance in the study of family history. If a town record is found of a warning to certain persons to depart from the town, and the statute under which the warning must have been given to be effective fixes the period within which such warning must have been made at three months, it may be fairly assumed that the persons came into the town at a time not earlier than three months before the warning was given. Frequently also these warning out notices were issued to families and gave the names of the different members of the family, so that from them it may be fairly assumed that the names comprised all the members of the family. Generally, also, the members of the family are named in the order of their ages, beginning with the father and mother, and then naming from the oldest to the youngest child, so that the respective ages of the children may be fairly assumed therefrom. In some cases these notices state the place from which the person or persons came into the town, although this is not general in such warn-

---
*Bellingham v. Boylston, 4 Cush. 553.
Leicester v. Fitchburg, 7 Allen, 90.

ings. In a few cases it will be found that the records of the warning out notices state the occupation of the persons warned, and in all cases the records show the names of the selectmen or persons who issued warrants for warnings, of the constables who served them, and of the town clerk who recorded them on the books of the town, thus in some cases giving information not otherwise obtainable from the town records.

If we judge these warning out statutes by the standards of the present time, they seem to have been strange and unjust. Now that persons are at liberty to move into and live in any municipality, we cannot quite understand why it was either necessary or right to exclude them from coming into and living in any town in the old times, nor can we understand why, if persons did come into any town and make it their home, they could properly be deprived of the benefit of being relieved by the town in case they became poor and in need of help.

But if we consider the condition in which the early settlers were placed, and especially the fact that each town was by the ancient law responsible for the support of such of its inhabitants as became poor and in need of help, we see that this obligation, as well as the obligation of the towns at that time for the good conduct of their inhabitants, made it necessary that the towns should be able to exclude from inhabitancy persons whom they did not desire to receive as inhabitants.

This was the fundamental law underlying the establishment of towns in New England, and was the only rule upon which in the sparsely settled condition of the country at that time the poor could be provided for at first. The towns were united into effective colony and State government by slow degrees, as

Warning Out in New England 119

roads and bridges were built, means of intercommunication were opened between the towns, and trade and commerce increased throughout the colonies and the early States. The only efficient method of taking care of the poor at that time was by requiring the towns to take care of them. In the very beginning the towns were able to exclude persons from inhabitancy whom they did not want by refusing to give them lands, and by refusing to allow those to whom lands had been granted to sell them to others whom the towns did not wish to admit as inhabitants. Later the towns sought to protect themselves against liability for the support of new inhabitants by requiring them to give security, usually by a bond from some other persons, to indemnify the town if it should ever be required to support the new-comers. This was carried so far that physicians to whom persons from out of the town came for treatment were required to become responsible to the town for any liability to support such persons if they became poor. But, as the population increased and means of communication multiplied, people came into towns and lived, and became inhabitants in spite of these precautions.

People came into towns notwithstanding these restraints and without giving security. Some of them became "sick or lame" to use the language of the law of the time, and they needed help. How were they to be helped? The colony law said: "The towns must help them. If the towns admit people as inhabitants, they must take care of them if they need help." The towns said: "We have not admitted them. They have come in without our consent. We do not want them, but we cannot keep them out, and there is no way by which we can effectively protect ourselves against liability for their support if they come in. The burden is likely to be too great for us to bear in many towns." Then it was provided by colony law that, if the towns warned new-comers to depart within three months after they came into them, the towns should be under no liability for their support, but they should be supported at the expense of the colony if they came to need support. The towns soon complained that three months was too short a period within which to warn out new-comers, because knowledge of their coming in did not in all cases come to the towns during that time. Then the colony law was changed to make the period within which the new-comer could be warned out twelve months, and, to make it certain where the responsibility for the support of persons who might come to be in need was to rest, the law required that these warnings should be recorded on the books of the towns or on the records of the court.

These warning out statutes were, as it will be seen, only a step in the economic development of the colony and the state from a condition where towns could practically exclude new-comers, and therefore ought to be responsible if they did not, to a condition where they could not practically exclude them, and, therefore, ought not to be held responsible simply because such persons came to live in the towns. The statutes were a part of the growth of the poor-laws of New England, which were afterwards put into form in the various settlement acts or laws of which I have spoken, providing how settlements could be obtained in towns.

There was a reason for these warning out statutes and for warning people out under them. The people were poor, the towns were sparsely populated, their people for a long time had little property, if any, except that which they produced from the soil or wrested from the sea. The average well-to-do person prior to 1800 did not have an estate equal to more than $750 at the present time. I do not mean by this the average of all persons, but the average of all persons who were considered well off. These people were naturally unwilling to be burdened with the responsibility of support for anybody who might come into the town, whether responsible or irresponsible. In addition to this there was at that time a large emigration of poor people from the Old World, and there was the flotsam and jetsam of a degenerate population coming up from the islands of the New World and flocking into the towns and villages of New England. It was right that these persons should become chargeable to the colony rather than to the towns. Warning out accomplished this purpose, and these statutes, as applied to the conditions under which they were passed, were reasonable and proper.

CHRONOLOGY.

1497.	Cabots' Discovery of North America.
1583.	Gilbert's Possession of Newfoundland.
1601.	First English Poor Law.
1602.	Gosnold landed in New England.
1606.	James I., Virginia Patent.
1620.	James I., Grant to "Council established at Plymouth, in the County of Devon, for the Planting, Ruling, and Governing of New England in America."
1629.	Charles I. grants Massachusetts Bay Charter.
1629.	Charles I. grants New-Plimouth Charter.
1631.	Grant to Connecticut Colony.
1638.	Roger Williams's Settlement in Rhode Island.
1671.	First Plymouth Warning Out Law.
1673.	First Connecticut Warning Out Law.
1692.	First Massachusetts Warning Out Statute.
1718.	First Warning Out Act in New Hampshire.
1787.	First Warning Out Act in Vermont.
1793.	First Massachusetts Settlement Act.
1796.	First Connecticut Settlement Act.
1796.	First Settlement Act in New Hampshire.
1817.	First Vermont Settlement Act.
1821.	First Settlement Act in Maine.

INDEX.

Act of Settlement, see Settlement Act.
Adams, Samuel, admitted, 36.
Admission of inhabitants, see Inhabitancy.
Aldrich, Levi, constable at Littleton, N.H., 95.
"Allotters," meaning of, 19.
Alstead, N.H., warning out in, 1, 98.
Andover, Mass., admission and inhabitancy in, 37.
Antrim, N.H., warning out in, 97.
Aquidneck, R.I., town compact of, 99.
Arnoll, Edw., 22.
Articles of Confederation of 1672 recognize right of towns to warn out, 49, 114.
Aspewall, William, fined, 20.
Attleboro, Mass. (1697), vote as to warning out, 57.
Average wealth of well-to-do people prior to 1800, 120, 121.
Avoidance of effect of warning out, 116, 117.

Bale, Frances, fined, 41.
Balstone, William, 20.
Barrill, George, cooper, 21.
Barron, Jonathan, selectman of Rockingham, Vt., 2.
Beamsle(a)y, William, 25.
Belfast, Me., warning out in, 102.
Bellingham, Richard, bondsman, 23.
Bellows, Fanny A., daughter; George and Henry Adams, sons; Mary, wife of Joseph Bellows, 2, 3.
Bellows, Joseph, and family, warned out, 2, 3.
Bellows Falls, Vt., 112.
Bennett, John, 86.
Benton, Jacob, and family, warned out, 1–3.
Benton, Hannah, wife; Jacob, Jr., Reynold, and Samuel, sons; Mabel and Mary, daughters of Jacob Benton, 1, 2.
Bernardston, Mass., warning out cases in 1790, 62.
Bill, Dorothie, a widowe, 21.
Billerica, Mass., admission to inhabitancy in, 35.
Bird, Thomas, 40.
Black, Mr. ——, warned out, 27.
Blague, Henry (or William), bondsman, 24.
Blesdale, Elizabeth, admitted, 25.
Blore, Jeams, warned out, 84.
Boston, Mass.: admission upon security, 23; allotments to newcomers and conditions of inhabitancy, 19–21; church relations of early settlers, 22; fines imposed for entertaining persons without consent of town, 23, 24; first case on record of support of persons admitted, 24; general order (1659) concerning entertainment of persons not admitted as inhabitants, 25; liability of town for support of persons admitted, 21; right of commonage restricted (May 18, 1648), 10; strangers to be reported to selectmen within 8 days, 22, 23.
Bracton quoted, 5, 6.
Bradford, William, and associates, receive grant of New Plymouth, 17.
Bradice, Ralph, admitted, 40.
Braintree, Mass., inhabitancy and warning out in, 34.
Bridge, John, 61.
Bridgewater, Mass., custom of warning out in, 62.
Bridgman, James, 41.
Brooks, Joe, 85.
Brooks, Simon, Jr., selectman of Alstead, N.H., 2.
Brown, Daniel, constable at Lexington, Mass., 61.
Brown, John, warned out, 43.
Bruff, William, admitted, 23.
Bullock, Henry, 29.
Burges, Francis, 23.
Burrill, George, cooper, fined, 24.

Index

Cabot, John and Sebastian, discovery of North America (1497), 12, 14; receive English royal grants in 1495, 14.
Cambridge, then Newtowne, admission to inhabitancy, etc., 30–32.
Camden, Me., warning out in, 103.
Canton, Mass., on warning out, 58.
Castine, Me., warning out in, 103.
"Caution," meaning of, 60.
Chapin, Henry, 28.
Chapin, Josiah, 28.
Chapin, ——, deacon, 28.
Charles I, grants Massachusetts Bay charter, 17; grants New Plymouth charter, 17.
Charlestown, Mass., admission to inhabitancy and entertainment of strangers in, 29.
Charlton, Robert, selectman of Littleton, N.H., 96.
Chelmsford, Mass., inhabitancy in, 35, 36.
Cheney, William, bondsman, 43.
Child, Saml, caution entered against, 60.
Chronological table, 122.
Chub, Mercy, warned out, 42.
Chub, Thomas, of Beuerlee, 42.
Church communion and right to vote in Massachusetts Colony, 8.
Church relations of early settlers, 22.
Cole, Samuell, fined, 20.
Collins, the widow, 39, 40.
Colony and Province of Providence, see Rhode Island.
Colored persons, Connecticut Act to prevent the setting up of schools for the instruction of, 81.
Commonage, right of, and restrictions, 10.
Connecticut: Act against colored schools, 81; admission upon surety in, 87; and Indian land titles, 13; colony law (1659) on restraint of alienation of lands to strangers, and warning out, 18, 114, 115; first warning out law (1673), 65; franchise in, 8; granted in 1630 to Robert, Earl of Warwick, 17; history of land titles in, 11, 12; inhabitancy and warning out in, 63–87, 114–115; Settlement Act (1796), 74–80, 115; provisions of Act now in force, 82.
Cononicus and Miontinomi, Indian chiefs, 99.
Cook, Sarah, caution entered against, 60.
Corbee, Goodman, 84.
Cornnell, Thomas, 20.
Cornwall, Vt., custom of warning out, 111.
Council, The, established at Plymouth, in the County of Devon, for the Planting, Ruling, and Governing of New England in America, 16, 17.
Crowe, Mr. ——, committeeman at Yarmouth, 44.
Crown grants and land titles, 11, 12.
Culberson, Jean, warned out, 96.
Cullymore, Isaacke, carpenter, fined, 20.
Cunningham, Thomas, selectman of Peterboro, N.H., 96.
Curtice, Isack, 85.
Curtice, Richard, 40.
Cutting, Daniel, and wife, caution entered against, 60.

Dauenport, ——, Lieft:, mentioned, 32.
Davis, Elias, warned out, 103.
Davis, John, 35.
Dedham, Mass., inhabitancy and warning out in, 32, 33; land controversy with Indians, 12, 13.
Deerfield, Mass., inhabitancy in, 56.
District of Maine, see Maine.
Dix, Edmand, caution entered against, 61.
Dorchester, Mass., inhabitancy conditions in, 38–43; restriction of right of commonage, 10, 11.
Doten, Zepheniah, and family, warned out, 45.
Dudley, Mass., records on warning out, 58.
Durham, Me., warning out in, 103.
Duxbury, Mass., inhabitancy conditions in, 43.
Dyer, Paul, warned out, 103.

Index 125

Early colony and state laws as to inhabitancy and warning out in Connecticut, 63–83; Maine, 104–106; Massachusetts, 46–53; New Hampshire, 88–95; Plymouth Colony, 53–55; Rhode Island, 99–101; Vermont, 106–110.
Eaton, of Thomaston, Me., statement by, 102, 103.
"Eaton's Code" (1655) and provisions as to inhabitancy, 87.
Effect of warning out, how avoided, 116, 117.
Eives, Joseph, 85.
Ellens, Danil, 41.
Ely, Samuel, admitted, 28.
Endecott, John, charter member of the Massachusetts Bay Colony, 17.
Enfield, Conn., order regarding sale of land, 84.
England, admission to inhabitancy on same conditions as in New England, 26, note*; legal inhabitancy in, 9; poor relief in mediæval, 7, 8.
English: civil institutions and law, basis of, 6; common law and warning out in New England, 4, 5; local and municipal development traced, 6, 7,
Estabrook, Capt. Joseph, 60.
Everson, John, warned out, 37.
Examples of warning out, *see* Warning out.
Exeter, N.H., on inhabitancy, 88; practice of warning out in, 97, 98.

Fair(e)ban(c)k(e), Richard, 19, 20.
Family history greatly aided by town records of warnings out and the statutes by which they were authorized, 117.
Fees to town officers produced by the process of warning out, 111, 112.
Finch, Mrs. ——, of West Chester, 87.
First case: of support by town of Boston of person admitted, 24; of warning out in New England, 23.
First great poor law in England, 8.

First Settlement Act, *see* Settlement Act.
First warning out Act in New Hampshire (1718), 89; in Vermont (1787), 106, 107.
First warning out law in Connecticut (1673), 65; in Plymouth Colony (1671), 59.
First warning out statute in Massachusetts (1692), 51.
Fletcher, Timo., selectman of Alstead, N.H., 2.
"Followers," meaning of, 6.
Foote, Good^n, admitted, 85.
Ford, Timothy, admitted, 29.
Foreigners and inhabitancy in Connecticut, 78.
Foule, Thomas, admitted, 21.
"Frankpledge," meaning of, 5, 6.
Free fishing and fowling, right of, 10.
Freedom of the community, *see* Inhabitancy.
Fryar, Nat., bondsman, 24.
Fundamental articles of agreement in Woodbury, Conn., 86.
"Fundamentals," The, so called, of Connecticut, 63, 64.
Funnell, Mrs. ——, 41, 42.

Galloppe, John, 20.
Garish, Nathaniel, selectman of Durham, Me., 104.
Gates, Sir Thomas, and others, receive patent for Colony of Virginia, 16.
General Court of the Massachusetts Colony, orders and laws of the, regarding inhabitancy and warning out, 46–52.
Generall Lawes & Liberties of the Province of New Hampshire (16$\frac{79}{80}$) on the exclusion of strangers, 88.
Gilbert, Sir Humphrey, 12, 14; receives patent from Queen Elizabeth, 15; takes possession of Newfoundland, 15.
Gilbert, Jno., 24.
Gilford, William, brikelayer, admitted, 23.
Gillam, Robert, marryner, admitted, 20.
"Giving the freedom of the city," effective meaning of, 9.

Index

Gleison, Thomas, warned out, 31, 32.
Gorges, Sir Ferdinando, 16.
Gorham, Me., warning out in, 102.
Gornell, John, bondsman, 40.
Gosnold visits Massachusetts Bay (1602), 15.
Governor and Company of the Massachusetts Bay in Newe-England, 17.
Grants of land by towns, 18.
Greene, Peter, 41.
Greenefield, Mr. ——, 20.
Greenfield, Mass., warning out cases in, 62.
Gregg, Hugh, selectman of Peterboro, N.H., 96.
Groton, Mass., inhabitancy and warning out in, 33.
Guilford, Conn., decision on sale or purchase of land, 84.
Gunn, Thomas, 86.

Haddam, Conn., warning out in, 84.
Hadley, Mass., inhabitancy and warning out in, 37.
Hall, Isaac, 28.
Harmon, Daniel, of Standish, warned out, 103.
Hart, John, fined, 24.
Hartford, Conn., orders as to receiving or warning out newcomers, 83.
Hartford, Vt., practice of warning out in, 111.
Harvard, John, and others, admitted as inhabitants in Charlestown, 29.
Harwood, Thomas, bondsman, 23.
Hatch, Ansal, selectman of Littleton, N.H., 96.
Haverhill, Mass., all new-comers warned out in, 60.
Hayden, William, 86.
Heard, Edmund, and family, warned out, 2, 3.
Henniker, N.H., warning out in, 96.
Henry, John, 56.
Hickock, Nath'l, 85.
Hims,——,widdow, warned out, 40.
Hodge, Ann, caution entered against, 61.

Holmes, Debora, refused admission, 32.
Holyoke, Elizur, bondsman, 28.
House ownership very desirable for admission to inhabitancy, 22.
Howes, Mr. ——, committeeman of Yarmouth, 44.
Hoyden, James, admitted, 29.
Hudson, Charles, statement as to warning out in Lexington, Mass., 60–62.
Hudson, William, fined, 20.
Hull, Elizabeth, wife of Roberte Hull, 22.
Hull, Richard, carpenter, 20.
Hutchinson, Ralph, fined, 24.
Hutchinson, Richard, warned out, 61.

Illustrations of warning out, see Warning out.
Immigration into New England, a cause of the warning out practice, 121.
Indian deeds and original land titles, 12, 13; wars (1675) and warning out, 50.
Inhabitancy: and warning out, 8; conditions of admission to, 18, 19; early colony and state laws, 46–55, 63–83, 88–95, 99–101, 104–110; historic basis of, 5; implies right to lands and commonage, 10; legal, in England, 9; right and obligations of, in Boston, 19–23; Connecticut, 63–87; Maine, 101–106; Massachusetts towns, outside of Boston, 26–37; New England, 4–19; New Hampshire, 88–98; Plymouth Colony, 37–46; Rhode Island, 99–101; Vermont, 101–113.
Inhabitants of other States than Connecticut, statutes concerning admission of, 78–82.

Jackson, John, fined, 43.
James I, gives Virginia patent (1602), 16; charter to "The Council established at Plymouth, in the County of Devon, for the Planting, Ruling, and Governing of New England in America" (1620), 16.

Index

Johnson, James, warned out, 103.
Johnson, Peter, the Dutchman, 20, 21.
Jordan, Samuel and Jedediah, warned out, 103.

Keniston, Mrs. ——, admitted, 32.
Kettle, Richard, mentioned, 29.
Kidder, Saml., constable of Alstead, N.H., 1, 2.
Knight, Elijah, selectman of Rockingham, Vt., 113.

Lancaster, Mass., cases of warning out in 1791, 2, 3; forms of warning out used in 1671, 56; inhabitancy and warning out, 33.
Land, restraint of alienation of, 18, 19.
Land ownership and inhabitancy in New England, 11.
Land titles in New England, origin of, 10–17.
Lane, Op'tunitie Lane, 43.
Langham, Mary, 24.
Length of time warning out was effective and practised, 114–116, 120.
Lewes, John, fined, 23.
Lexington, Mass., warning out in, 60.
Littleton, N.H., practice of warning out in, 95, 96.
Long, Joseph, 40.
Lyall, Francis, admitted, 20.
Lynn, Mass., orders of warning out in, 59.
Lyon, Petter, 41.

MacKentiah, Martha, of Reading, warned out, 58.
Mackintosh, Archable, and family, warned out, 61.
Mackreth, Reginald, from Liverpool in Nova Scotia, warned out, 45.
Mahoney, Mrs. ——, and child, warned out, 59.
Mahoone, Derman, fined, 24, 25.
Maine: and land titles, 14; Constitution of, October 29, 1819, 104; Settlement Act (1821), 104, 105, 115; town settlement, inhabitancy, relief of poor and warning out in, 101–106, 115.

Man, Kezia, caution entered against, 60.
Maps and charts, early, of American coast, 14, 15.
March, Abigail, Hannah, Prudence, and Sarah, children of Samuel and Tabatha March, 112.
March, Samuel, wife and children, warned out, 112, 113.
March, Tabatha, wife of Samuel March, 112, 113.
Marcy, Moses, Esq., 60.
Marshfield, Mass. (1664), on inhabitancy and warning out, 55.
Marten, Thomas, warned out, 84.
Mason, Captain John, 16; vested rights of, 14.
Massachusetts: early colony and state laws regarding inhabitancy and warning out, 46–53; first warning out statute (1692), 51, 114; Settlement Act (1793), 55, 114; warning out cases in 1794, 52, 53, 114.
Massachusetts Bay charter granted by Charles I (1629), 17.
Massachusetts Colony, right of voting in, 8, 9.
Mawer, William, 20.
Maxfild, Clement and John, 39.
Maynard, John, and family, warned out, 2, 3.
Medfield, Mass., inhabitancy and warning out in, 34.
Medford, Mass., custom of warning out in, 57.
Me(i)lton, Mass., mentioned, 40, 41.
Merrifeild, Henery, 41, 42.
Merrye, Water, 22.
Middleboro, Mass., inhabitancy conditions in, 38.
Miller, Simon, 86.
Ministers, settlement of settled and ordained, in Maine Act of Settlement, 105; in Massachusetts Act, 53, 116, 117.
Miontinomi, see Cononicus.
Morgan, Quartus, selectman of Rockingham, Vt., 113.
Morse, John, admitted, 29.
Moses, John, 85, 86.
Muddy River, 21; (Brookline) a "peculiar," 49, note *.

Municipalities' liability for property destroyed in riots, origin of, 9.
Mylne feild, Boston, mentioned, 22.

Naticke, Mass., Indians of, and sales of land, 13.
Newbury, Mass., warning out in, 59.
Newbury, Vt., practice of warning out new-comers, 111.
New-comers to new towns, usually warned out as a caution, 46–62, 119, 120, and *passim*.
New England: admission of inhabitants, 18; first record of warning out in, 23; origin of land titles in, 10–17; original dimensions of, 16; poor laws the outgrowth of the warning out statutes, 120; right and obligations of inhabitancy, 4–9; right of exclusion from, exercised in the colonies, 10; settlers follow custom of English affairs, 8; warning out, examples of and reasons for, 1–4, 8.
Newfoundland, settlement at (1522), 15; taken possession of by Gilbert, 15.
New France, 15.
New Hampshire: first warning out Act (1718), 89; inhabitancy and warning out in, 88–98, 115; royal province of, and land titles, 14; Settlement Act (1796), 115.
New Haven, Conn., admission to and inhabitancy in, 86, 87.
New Plymouth, Colony of, *see* Plymouth Colony.
Newport, R.I., order as to sale of land, etc., by General Court, 100.
Newtowne, *see* Cambridge.
Northampton, Mass. (1672), and land titles, 13.
Norton, Francis, admitted, 29.

Olcott, Elias, selectman of Rockingham, Vt., 2.
Oliuer, Frances, warned out, 40.
Osgood, Aaron, selectman of Durham, Me., 104.
Oxford, Mass., warning out (1789 foll.) in, 62.

Painter, Thomas, 21.
Palmer, John, carpenter, 22.
Pane, Mr. ——, of Concord, 21.
Parish, becomes the poor-law unit, 7, 8; original function of, 6, 7; revival of importance of (1601), 8.
Parker, Jonathan, Jr., constable of Rindge, N.H., 97.
Parker, Richard, merchant, admitted, 21.
Patch, Samuel, 58.
Pawtuxet River, R.I., 99.
Peacepledge, meaning of, 5, 6.
Pease, John, bondsman, 24.
Peculiar, 49, 54; meaning of, 49, note *.
Penobscot, Me., warning out in, 103.
Pequot territory, 13.
Perry, Arthure, 22.
Peterboro, N.H., warning out in, 96.
Pighogg, a Chururgeon; admitted, 23.
Pingree, Eben, selectman of Littleton, N.H., 96.
Pittman, Richard, first person warned out in New England (1656), 23.
Plum, John, and Mercy Chub, his daughter, 42.
Plymouth Colony and town: and land grants, 14; charter granted by Charles I (1629), 17; early colony laws as to inhabitancy, 53–55; first warning out law (1671), 54; franchise in, 8; inhabitancy conditions in, 37, 38, 44.
Poland, Margaret, widow, 58.
Poor law in England, the first great (1601), 8.
Poor laws in New England, origin of, 120.
Poor relief in colonial New England, 118, 119; in mediæval England, 7, 8.
Pope, John, 41.
Portsmouth, R.I., inhabitancy order of, 100.
Proctor, Samuel, of Plymouth, warned out, 103.
"Proprietors" and grants of land, 17.

Index

Providence, R.I., compact for the establishment of, 99, 100.
Province of New Hampshire, *see* New Hampshire.
Prudential men = the selectmen, 48.
Pryor, Daniel, of Tewksbury, warns himself out, 59.
Pulsipher, Sam'l W., selectman of Rockingham, Vt., 2.

Raleigh, Sir Walter, first to occupy Virginia, 15, 16.
Rand, Goodman, admitted, 29.
Rawlings, Richard, a plasterer, 20.
Read, Elijah, constable at Rockingham, Vt., 113.
Reade, Esdras, taylor, 21.
Reading, Mass. (1691), cases of warning out in, 57.
Reasons for warning out summarized, 118.
Restraint upon alienation of land, 18, 19.
Revolutionary War causes greater stringency as to warning out, 56 foll., 62, 73, 94, 98, 101, 103, 111.
Rhode Island: and Indian land titles, 13; early colony and state laws as to inhabitancy and warning out, 99–101; history of land titles in, 11, 12; inhabitancy, relief of poor, town settlement, etc., 99–101; warning out never authorized by statute, 115.
Rice, Merrick, warned out, 3.
Rindge, N.H., warning out in, 96.
Rise, Isack, and Nehimia Rise, 85.
Rix, ———, widow, refused inhabitancy, 86.
Robbe, Alexr., selectman of Peterboro, N.H., 96.
Robbins, James, 61.
Roberson, Daniel, warned out, 103.
Robert, Earl of Warwick, 16, 17.
Roberts, Henery, warned out, 41.
Rockingham, Vt., warning out in, 2, 112.
Roff, Daniel, and family, warned out, 61.
Rosewell, Sir Henry, charter member of the Massachusetts Bay Colony, 17.

Ross, Hannah, caution entered against, 61.
Rourk, Martin, town clerk of Durham, Me., 104.
Rowley, Mass., inhabitancy and warning out in, 36.
Roxbury, Mass., warning out in, 38.
Russian communities and restraint of alienation of lands, 18.

Saco, Me., inhabitancy and warning out in, 34, 35.
Salem, Mass., inhabitancy and warning out in, 32, 36; cases of warning out in 1679 and 1695, 56.
Saltonstall, Sir Richard, charter member of the Massachusetts Bay Colony, 17.
Sampson, Elizabeth, widow, of Harvard, Mass., 61.
Sandwich, warning out in, 37.
Sanford, Me., warning out in, 102.
Sanfurd, Richard, 24.
Saunders, Silvester, 22.
Saunders, ———, a booke-bynder, 20.
Scituate, Mass., inhabitancy and warning out in, 26.
Seaberry, John, a seaman, admitted, 22.
Seaborne, John, a taylor, admitted, 21.
Searle, Phillip, 41.
Security, admission upon, 23, 87, and *passim;* bond of, ordinarily twenty pounds, 25.
Settlement Act: in Connecticut (1796), 74–80, 115; and provisions of Act now in force, 82; Maine (1821), and its provisions differing from the Massachusetts Act, 104, 105, 115; Massachusetts (1793), 52, 53, 55, 114; New Hampshire (1796), 115; Vermont, (1817), 113, 115.
Seward, Richard, admitted, 24.
Shepard, Amos, selectman of Alstead, N.H., 2.
Sherman, Philip, 20.
Sled, John, and wife, warned out, 84.
Smith, Jeremiah, warned out, 103.
Smith, Quince, 28.
Smith, Ralph, admitted, 29.

Index

Smith, Richard, admitted, 24.
Snellen, ——, Dr., of Boston, 42.
Snow, Johanna, caution entered against, 60.
Sowers, Roger, 23.
Spencer, Jarrad, 83, 84.
Spencer, Roger, 34, 35.
Sprague, Hon. John, and family, warned out, 2, 3, 56.
Springfield, Mass., admission to inhabitancy and entertainment of strangers under strict control, 27, 28.
Squakeage, village of, 13.
Stackpole, John, warned out, 103.
Stearns, Ezra S., historian, statement by, 97.
Stedman, John, bondsman, 84.
Stedman, William, warned out, 3.
Steuens, child of Mr. ——, of Boston, 43.
Stockbridge, Hannah, caution entered against, 61.
Stone, Abigail, of Woburn, 61.
Storer, Richard, admitted, 22.
Strangers: entertainment of strangers under strict control, 23–45 and *passim;* laws of General Court of Massachusetts as to admission of, 46–63; to be reported to selectmen within 8 days, 22, 23, and *passim.*
Sturbridge, Mass., 60.
Sudbury, Mass., warning out in, 57, 58.
Summary of reasons for warning out, 118–121.
Sumner, William, 40.
Surety, admission upon, *see* Security, admission upon.
Sutton, town of, 60.

Teffe, William, taylor, 21.
Templeton, James, constable of Peterboro, N.H., 96.
Tewksbury, Mass., some queer cases of warning out in, 59.
Thacher, Mr. ——, committeeman of Yarmouth, 44.
Thomas, Captain ——, 86.
Thomaston, Me., warning out in, 102.
Tilston, Timothy, bondsman, 41.

Tilstone, ——, constable at Plymouth, 41.
Tinge, Mr. ——, 20.
Tingle, Paletiah, warned out, 102.
Tithings, meaning and significance of Old English, 6.
Torrey, Ebenezer, and family, warned out, 2, 3.
Town, as defined by Blackstone, Coke, and others, 7.
Town vote avoids effect of warning out, 116.
Towns, right of, to warn out recognized by the Articles of Confederation (1672), 49.
Townsman and inhabitant, interchangeable terms, 21.
Tubbs, Zebulen, his wife Esther, and children, 56.
Turner, Ezekiel, of Freeport, warned out, 103.
Turner, ——, admitted, 29.
Tuttell, Richard, 21.

Underwood, Beulah, Junior Israel, Samuel, warned out, 95, 96.
Union, Me., warning out in, 102.

Value of warning out records, 117, 118.
Vermont: early colony and state laws as to inhabitancy and warning out, 106–110; first warning out Act in (1787), 106, 107; Settlement Act (1817), 111, 113, 115; town settlement, inhabitancy, relief of poor, and warning out, 106–113.
Vining, Benjamin, constable at Durham, Me., 103, 104.
Virginia, early history of colonial, 15, 16.
Voting privilege in Massachusetts Colony, 8, 9.

Waite, Abigail, warned out, 45.
Wales, Joseph, warned out, 3.
Wallingford, Conn., order as to admission, sales, etc., 84, 85.
Walpole, N.H., warning out in, 98.
Warning out: avoidance of effect of, by town vote, 116, 117; fees

Index 131

to town officers for, 111, 112; first record of, in New England, 23; historic basis of, 5; Indian wars and, 50; length of time of effectiveness of, 114–116, 120; never authorized by statute in Rhode Island, 115, 116; not provided by statute in State of Maine, 104, 105; notices of great importance for family and town history, 117, 118; reasons for, summarized, 118–121; Revolutionary War and, 56 foll., 62, 73, 94, 98, 101, 103, 111; right of towns to, recognized by Articles of Confederation, 49; Settlement Acts as to, 52, 53, 55, 74–86, 104, 105, 113–115; value of records of, 117, 118; wording of the returns of the warrants of, not uniform, 60.

Warning out in, Boston, 19–26; Connecticut, 63–87; Maine, 101–106; Massachusetts, 26–53; New England, 1–17; New Hampshire, 88–98; Plymouth, 44–62; Rhode Island, 99–101; Teutonic townships, 5; Vermont, 106–113.

Warrants of warning out, wording of the returns of the, not uniform, 60.

Warwick, Robert, Earl of, 16, 17.
Watters, Good^n, fined, 23.
Watertown, Mass., inhabitancy and warning out in, 33.
Way, Aron, 24.
Way, Richard, admitted, 24.
Wealth, average of, prior to 1800, 120, 121.

Web, Jno., ensigne, 24.
Weeks, Joseph, 43.
Wenbourne, William, 23.
Wenham, Mass., warning out in, 58.
Weymouth, Mass., inhabitancy and warning out in, 34.
Wheelwright and the Antinomians proceeded against, 47, 48.
Whipping in public, a punishment for disobeying notice of warning out, 66, 69–72, 76, 95 and *passim;* repealed in Connecticut, 80, 81.
Whittemore, Abigail, widow, 61.
Whittemore, Nathaniel, 61.
William, Viscount Say and Seal, 17.
Williams, Roger, 13, 99.
Williams, Thos, town clerk of Deerfield, Mass., 56.
Willson, Mr. Jno., senr., 24.
Wilson, Jacob, 21.
Windsor, Conn., 85.
Winthrop, John, first governor of Massachusetts, mentioned, 19.
Winthrop, John, the younger, surgeon at New Haven, Conn., and governor of the colony, 87.
Woburn, Mass., inhabitancy and warning out in, 26.
Wood, David, selectman of Rockingham, Vt., 113.
Wood, John, fined, 28.
Wo(o)dard, Nathaneell, admitted, 23.
Woodbury, Conn., fundamental articles of agreement, 86.
Worcester County, Mass., returns of warning out from the different towns of, 59, 60.
Wright, Richard, fined, 21.

www.ingramcontent.com/pod-product-compliance
Lightning Source LLC
Chambersburg PA
CBHW070919160426
43193CB00011B/1530